AF321484

LAURA KNIGHT

This book is from a series about Modern Women Artists
published by Eiderdown Books.

Other titles available from the same series:

To order books, please visit eiderdownbooks.com

LAURA KNIGHT

Alice Strickland

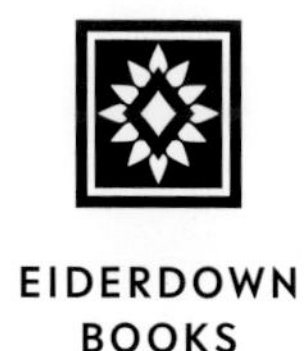

EIDERDOWN
BOOKS

MODERN WOMEN ARTISTS

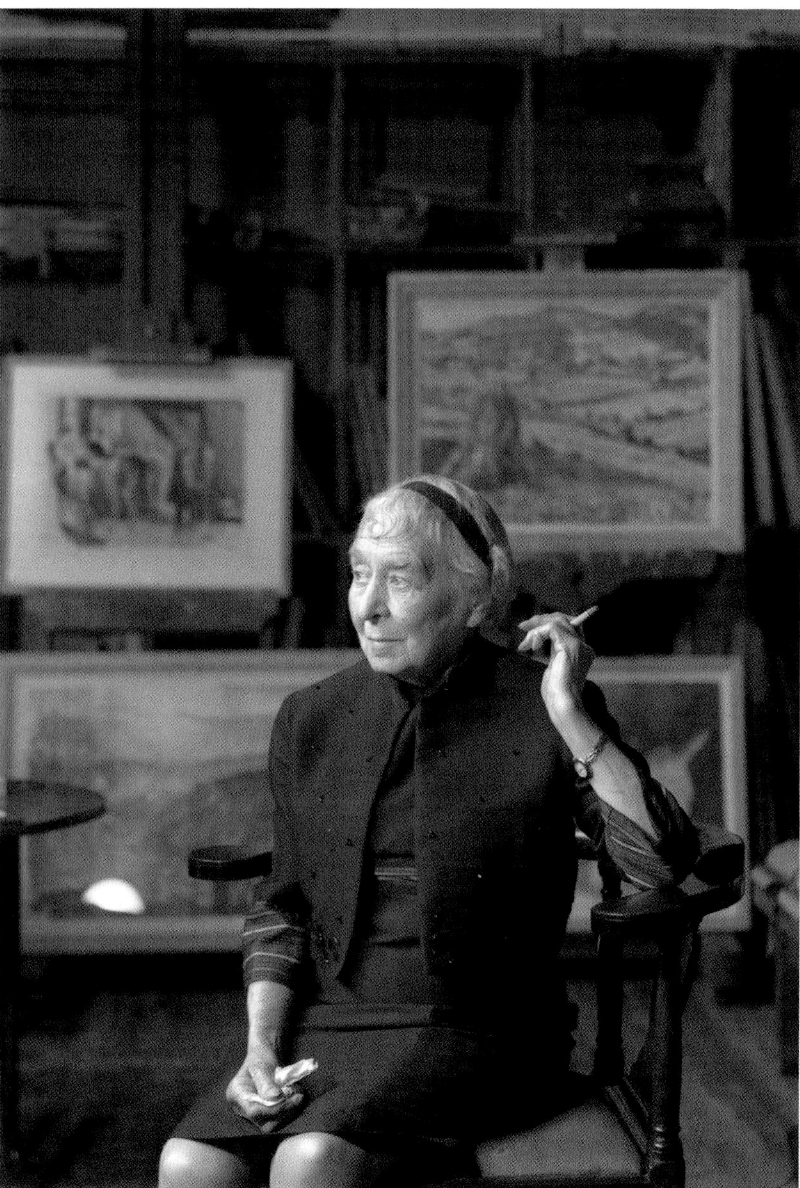

Painting, music, ballet, theatre, circus, art and physical skill, what joy to project oneself in each, to feel the daring of the acrobat, the control of the artist, in understanding and sympathy to live many lives in one![1]

Laura Knight (1877–1970) was one of the most highly regarded female artists of her generation (Fig. 1). From humble beginnings, she forged a successful career, becoming the first female artist to be made a Dame of the British Empire in 1929, and in 1936 became the first woman to be elected as a Royal Academician. Throughout her prolific career, spanning over 70 years, Knight was fascinated with depicting the places she visited and the people she met. An inveterate recorder of contemporary life and culture, she captured an extensive variety of subjects, including ballet dancers, circus performers, gypsies and war workers. She travelled with the circus and ballet and immortalised the lives of those who were part of such bohemian circles in a period of societal conformity.

Much of Knight's work vividly depicts the intimate and private world of women, as well as the life of the ballet and theatre. Her art was popular, insightful, intimate and brilliant. Her technical abilities, in a wide range of media, mixed sparkling innovation with academic rigour. As an important contributor to British twentieth-century culture, Knight's life and work deserve to be championed afresh.

1. Dame Laura Knight, 1967. Photograph by Madame Yevonde.

Early Life

Born on the 4 August 1877 in Long Eaton, Derbyshire, Laura Knight (née Johnson) entered the Nottingham School of Art in 1890. At a mere 13 years of age, she was probably the youngest pupil to have ever studied there. 'Through mother's influence I went straight into the Life Class, but for head and drapery only. Women were not allowed to draw from the nude.'[2] Knight's subsequent work shows none of the artistic limitations that this restrictive training, including a lack of access to depicting the nude, may have placed on her work. Throughout her career she showed both an eagerness to experiment with technique and to tackle new subjects, even searching them out, as shown in her depictions of gypsy life (see p.32).

By the end of the nineteenth century, types of feminine identity included the 'New Woman', a stereotype that drew upon those women who were now living independently and establishing careers as professionals. Thanks to her talent and hard work, Knight was able to establish herself as a professional artist and earn a living through her art; she was thus the embodiment of a new woman. While her work may not be considered 'modern', in the sense that she didn't exhibit with avant-garde groups, her work is modern in the way it depicted the contemporary world and ways in which that world was changing.

Mining the rich seams of Knight's work, the works illustrated here trace her role within the artistic communities in Laren and Cornwall, alongside her prolific and dedicated observation of marginalised communities and women at work (on stage, and later, during the Second World War). This essay seeks to demonstrate how Knight forged her way into the upper echelons of the art world alongside her male peers to become the first woman Royal Academician since Angelica Kauffmann (1741–1807) and Mary Moser (1744–1819). In a *Studio* magazine article of 1922, Knight wrote that women require equality of opportunity before they can succeed on the same terms as men.[3]

It was Knight's high professional profile that allowed her the opportunity to champion the work of fellow women artists. The Society of Female Artists, in 1899 renamed the Society of Women Artists (SWA), exhibited the work of Sylvia Gosse, Dod Procter and Knight, who became its first Honorary President in 1932. She retained this post until 1968.

By forming their own organisations such as the SWA and the Women's International Arts Club, women challenged discrimination and the exclusivity of established art institutions, creating their own opportunities for exhibiting and garnering patronage. Talking at an exhibition of women artists' work at Henley in 1933, Knight stated that while she believed 'it did not matter at all whether a picture was by a man or a woman … women do need some special encouragement from time to time.'[4]

Two years after she became a Royal Academician, the first of her two autobiographies, *Oil Paint & Grease Paint*, was published. One reviewer described it as being 'as vivid as her personality as vigorous and vital as are her pictures. The book is the woman.'[5] In 1965, a second autobiography, *The Magic of a Line*, was published to coincide with her Royal Academy (RA) retrospective of the same year. In this book Knight discusses her early life, stories of her family, her formative years in Nottingham and meeting fellow art student Harold Knight. In 1894, Knight visited Staithes, in North Yorkshire, with her aunt, sister and Harold. The following year Knight and her sister Sissie moved to Staithes, while Harold stayed in lodgings close by. On 3 June 1903 – the same year in which her first painting *Mother and Child* was hung at the RA – Knight and Harold were married in West Leake, and held the reception in East Leake, not far from Nottingham.

In 1904, Laura and Harold Knight first travelled to Holland, visiting Amsterdam and the artists' colony at Laren. They spent six months at Laren, while still based at Staithes, returning again in 1905 and 1906. In November 1907, the Knights moved to Newlyn, Cornwall and joined a circle of artists including Dod Procter and her husband Ernest. All becoming promoted to Royal Academicians alongside their close friends from the Newlyn School of Painting: AJ Munnings (President of the RA, 1944–9), John (Lamorna) Birch and Harold Harvey.

Munnings and Laura Knight remained close friends. Letters exchanged between them, archived at the RA, reflect the strong friendship and the relaxed manner between these artists. Although the earliest letter dates from 1942, they extend through and beyond Munnings' tenure as President of the RA, and provide insights into his relationship with the institution and its members. His notorious hatred of Modernism and its exponents, and his love of verse, is also evident in their correspondence. One of the leading traditional painters of his generation, Munnings was best known for his horse paintings at the races and depictions of gypsy encampments.

Knight's works from this period reflect her new life in Cornwall, and her dedication to painting *en plein air*; they encapsulate her refined interest in colour, light and form and their development into an Impressionist style that is distinctly British, evoking what has since become known as the 'long Edwardian summer'.

Cornwall Communities and Artistic Success

Following Knight's arrival in Newlyn she produced Impressionist Academy pieces such at *The Beach* (Fig. 2) and *Flying a Kite* (1910), depicting 'surroundings such as we had never dreamed of; a carefree life of sunlit pleasure.'[6] In *The Beach*, the figures of children are captured in the bright sunshine with the seascape acting as a backdrop to their activity. This period also coincided with one of financial success for Knight: 'Now there was no shortage of cash; both of us were doing well and I could sell nearly everything I touched, an exhilarating experience.'[7] Perhaps this allowed or even encouraged Knight to undertake her most artistically successful work – a bold study in composition

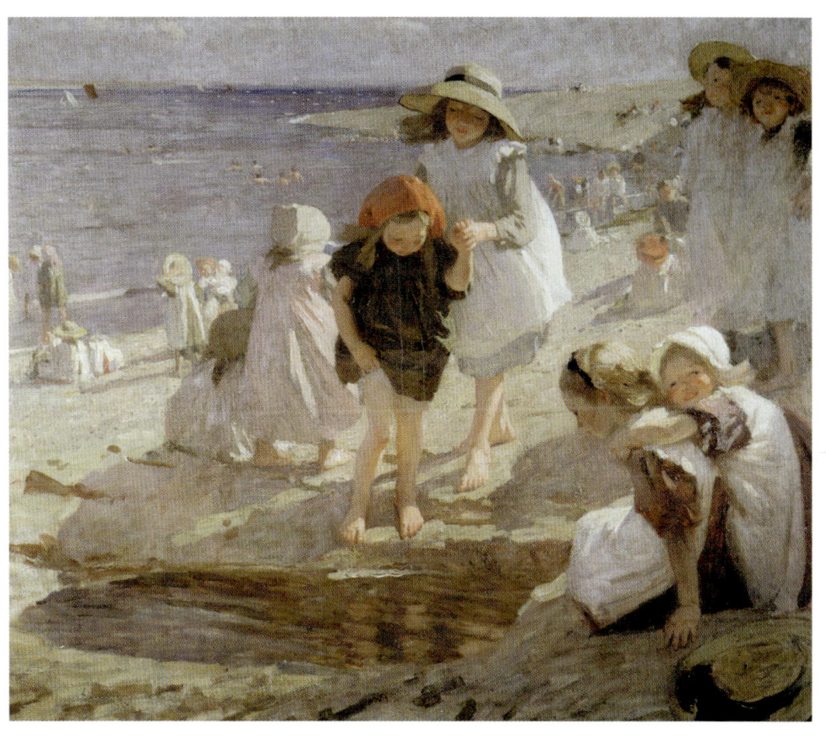

2. *The Beach*, c.1909, oil on canvas

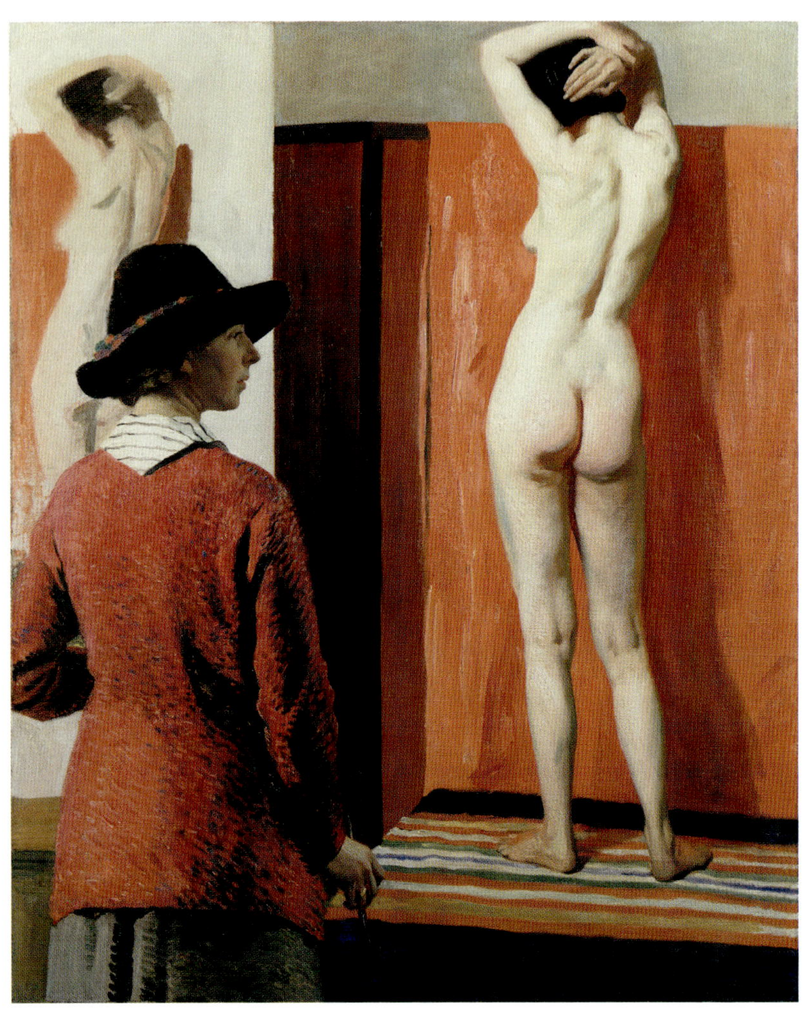

3. *The Model* or *Laura Knight with model, Ella Louise Naper ('Self Portrait')*, 1913, oil on canvas

and colour entitled *The Model* (Fig. 3). One reviewer, Herbert Thomas, wrote of the rapturous reception given to 'Mrs Knight's Triumph' on the first public showing of *The Model* at the Passmore Edwards Art Gallery, Newlyn Art Club: 'Place aux dames! And who will grudge Mrs Knight the honour? Certainly not her envious but loyal fellow-craftsmen. "Look at it!", cried one. There is not another woman in England – I doubt if there is another woman in the world – who could have painted that picture. It is, of course, an Exhibition picture – a tour de force!'[8]

At Nottingham School of Art, Knight had been denied access to the life room; now in Knight's new studio at Trethinnick, in the Lamorna Valley, the artist Ella Naper posed as the model on a dais. Consisting of three planes, the artist, the model and the canvas on which a further image of Ella appears, Knight creates a painting within a painting. She depicts the female form in a palette of reds and pinks, contrasting between flesh-coloured tones of the nude and the deep crimson red of Knight's knitted cardigan, all in a heavy impasto. The work's life-size dimensions make it a physically imposing work, and the viewer is captivated by Knight's gaze from beneath her black hat. In this work, Knight declares her artistic credentials and her mastering of the nude figure, and celebrates her friendship with Naper.

Knight's execution of this ambitious work challenges the historical confines of women artist's work. By the end of the nineteenth century, many women could train in the life room, but a major strand of Modernism had coalesced around the female model as a sign of the power, both creative and sexual, of the male artist. The list of male artists who focused on the female model during the early twentieth century is long, including most obviously, Henri Matisse, Pablo Picasso and Walter Sickert. In *The Model*, Knight sought to place herself within this visual tradition by depicting the female nude.

The painting was later exhibited at the International Society of Sculptors, Painters and Gravers in London. One reviewer considered it 'an extremely clever picture of a paintress and

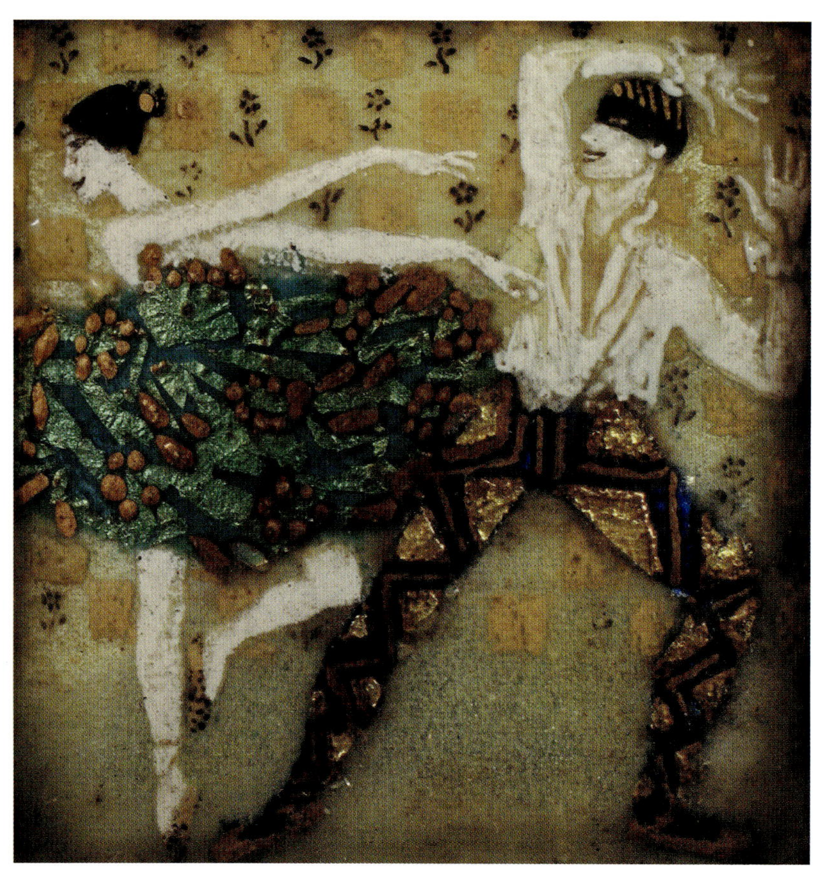

4. *Two Dancers*, 1915, oil on enamel

her model's back which, we fear, will provoke a smile not quite of admiration.'[9] More damning is the commentary by Claude Phillips in *The Daily Telegraph*:

> If only she has a spark of that imaginativeness which literally burns in the work of Mrs Swynnerton![10] Somehow, woman painting woman hardly ever infuses into her work the higher charm of the 'eternal feminine'. The painting is obviously but an exercise, and as such it might quite appropriately have stayed in the artist's studio. It repels . . . by dullness and by something dangerously near to vulgarity.[11]

Despite the reaction of some critics to the work, Knight continued to exhibit the painting throughout her career. Following Knight's death, the painting, now known as *Self Portrait* (1913), was purchased from her estate by the National Portrait Gallery, London, where it can still be seen today.

Knight and Naper both worked together on enamel works, including *Two Dancers* (Fig. 4). Both women had just moved to Lamorna, around the coast from the artist colony of Newlyn, living within a few hundred yards of each other. Shortly after its execution, the enamel was given by Laura and Harold Knight to fellow artists Charles and Ruth Simpson as a wedding present.

During the First World War, Knight remained predominantly in Cornwall, painting figures set against the Cornish coastline. *The Cornish Coast* (Fig. 5) depicts two of her regular Cornish models Phyllis Vipond-Crocker and Marjorie Taylor (left to right). Resting close by the models is Knight's Scottish terrier dog, Tip, who appears in a number of works from the period.

Naper appears again at the centre of Knight's large work *Spring* (Fig. 6), along with her husband Charles. The couple had arrived in Cornwall during 1912 and became good friends with the Knights. In *Oil Paint & Grease Paint*, Knight discusses the difficulty of working on *Spring* in the open air due to wartime restrictions:

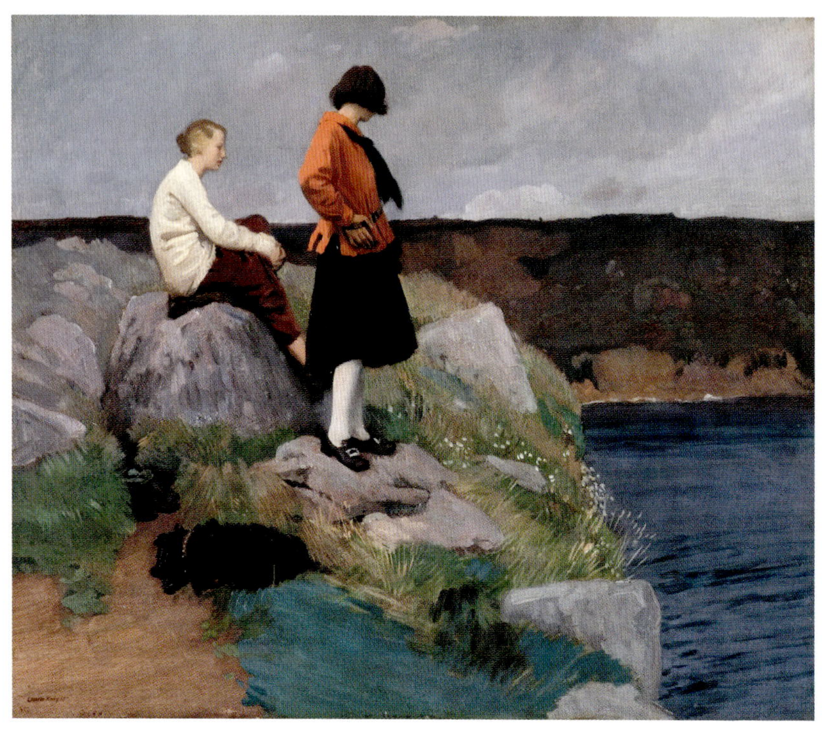

5. *The Cornish Coast*, 1917, oil on canvas

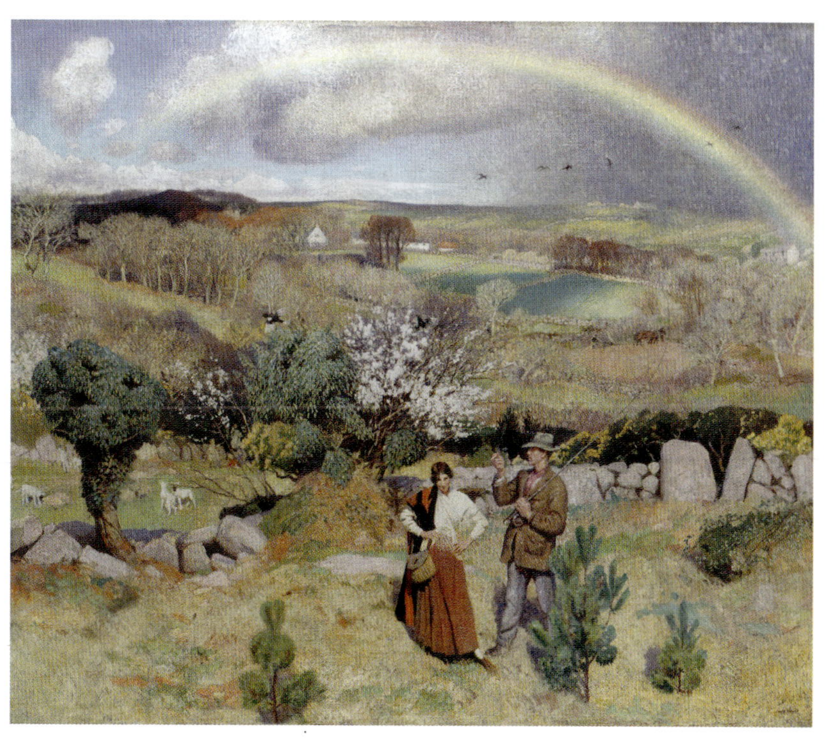

6. *Spring*, 1916–19, oil on canvas

This picture was painted during the World's War No. 1. At that time it was against the law to paint outdoors anywhere near the Cornish Coast. And to get the material I needed, here and there, I had to lie on my stomach under a gorse or any other convenient bush, in dread of being taken off to prison, to make a line or two in a sketch book, memorise – rush back into my studio, and paint.[12]

In spite of working conditions, the finished painting is a beautifully evocative picture of the Cornish countryside. Spring abounds, trees which line the meadows are about to burst into leaf, the lambs grazing with swifts flying above in the sky, a rainbow cutting into the scene perhaps a symbol of hope during a time of war. The rainbow also calls to mind Kauffmann's *Colour* (1778–80), one of four ceiling works, in which the artist takes her colour palette from the rainbow above.[13]

First World War Commission

During the two world wars, Knight undertook a variety of government-commissioned works. In 1916, she received a £300 commission to paint a canvas for the Canadian War Records Office, the brainchild of the Canadian-born newspaper magnate Sir Max Aitken (later Lord Beaverbrook), on the theme of 'Physical Training in a Camp'. Knight produced a series of studies, drawings and paintings on canvas of boxing matches at Witley, Surrey. In *Physical Training at Witley Camp* (Fig. 7), she represents Joe Shears of the 156th Canadian Infantry Battalion of the Canadian Expeditionary Force and his opponent Corporal W. Atkin set against a brooding sky. At the time, Shears was the Imperial Force's bantamweight champion.

Knight's commissions during the First World War played a significant role in her recognition as a professional artist of merit. In 1918, works from this period, as well as Knight's Cornish subjects, were included in *Camp Life* – a solo exhibition at the

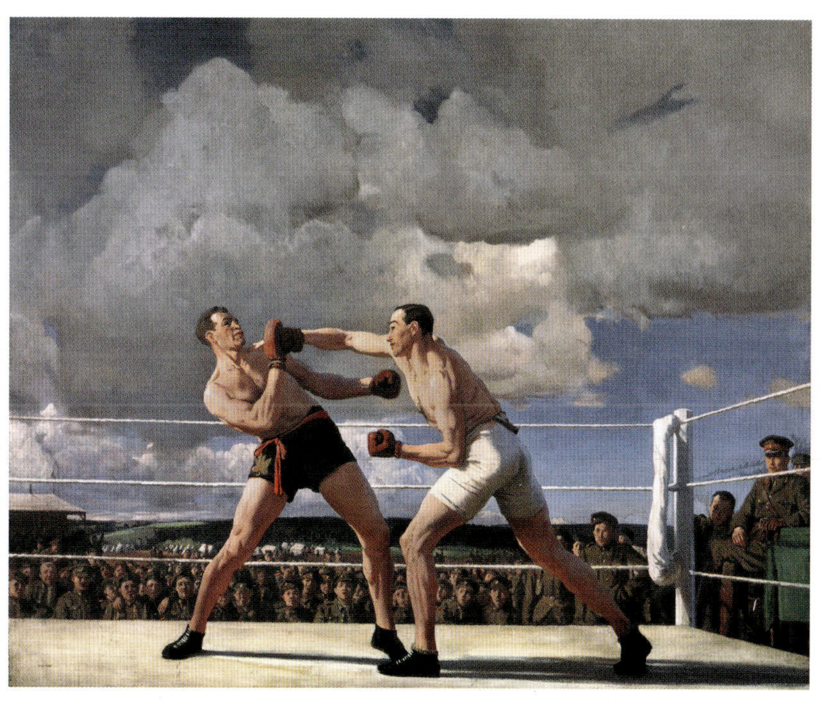

7. *Physical Training at Witley Camp*, c.1917, oil on canvas

Leicester Galleries, London, and later at the 1928 Summer Olympics in Amsterdam, Knight won the Silver Medal in Painting with her work *Boxer* (1917), from the Witley series.

In January 1919, following the First World War, Laura and Harold Knight left Cornwall for London, although Knight kept her Lamorna studio, and returned to Cornwall most summers. On moving to London, her wide circle of sitters now expanded to include the world of the ballet, circus, music and theatre.

The Ballets Russes

I firmly believe the most valuable study I have ever had was in my attempt to draw the ballet. Never before had I tried to make the pencil speak in a language all of its own.[14]

For 18 years from 1911, until the final London appearance of the Ballets Russes in 1929, Knight watched, drew and painted this visionary ballet company at every one of its London seasons, often backstage. The preparatory sketches for her ballet works, a number of which are in the collections of the RA and the Victoria and Albert Museum (V&A), demonstrate her working methods. Her sketches capture dancers at rest, their movement across the stage, the placement of each dancer as the ballet progresses and the poses they adopt, recording how they hold their arms, place their feet and heads.

Like many artists, Knight was captivated by the Ballets Russes during their first London season: 'I feel sorry for anyone who did not see Diaghilev's first seasons ... I can only say it gave me the feeling of being born into a new and glamorous world, with complete satisfaction for every aesthetic sense ... during the period when Pavlova and Karsavina were appearing in turn I saw every performance.'[15]

Her ballet works – particularly *Les Sylphides* (Fig. 8) – immediately call to mind the studies of dancers by Edgar Degas, often executed in pastel and thus vividly coloured. Knight's

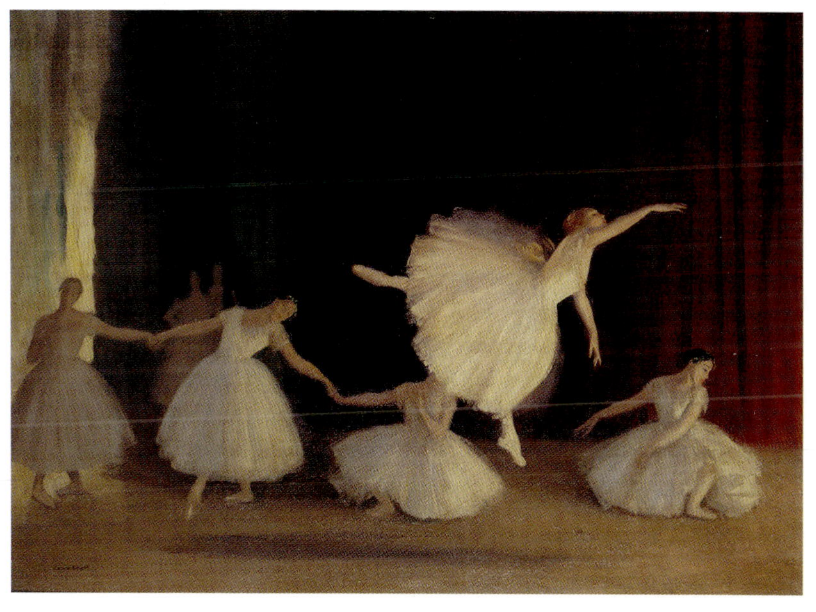

8. *Les Sylphides*, 1919, oil on canvas

manipulation of space, and figure-to-field relationships refer to Degas' paintings of ballet rehearsals, which she would have been familiar with via reproductions and exhibitions. The architecture of a picture by Degas, with its lines of perspective, intersection or mass delineation, in floor boards beneath dancers, in angles of mirrors, panels of doors, pillars and railings in rehearsal rooms, are also used effectively by Knight.

Anna Pavlova was one of the most famous ballerinas of her time (Fig. 9). Pavlova's dedication and tenacity impressed Knight as much as her dancing:

> How few realise the cost to the artiste, or what endurance and vital effort have gone to reach that pitch of perfection. Who among the audience could imagine their matchless ballerina hanging on to a curtain in the wings, panting, almost too tired to stand, with a stream of sweat pouring down her back? What pleasures others enjoy must she have denied herself to reach those heights![16]

In 1919, prima ballerina Lydia Lopokova offered Knight her dressing room as a studio at the Coliseum. Knight recalled their arrangement: 'Her room should be my studio, she should never stay in any position on my account, she should go on with her make-up and dressing, stand in front of the long glass and go through positions and steps. We were both workers. There was to be no conversation.'[17]

Knight's depictions of rehearsal studios, dressing rooms, the wings of the stage and curtain calls underline her privileged position, giving us an intimate insight into the world of ballet. By the early 1920s, she was beginning to make etchings in drypoint, depicting dancers with deep tones of aquatint, as illustrated in *Dressing Room No.1* (1923, Fig. 10). In this work, Lopokova sits in the foreground wearing striped pantaloons designed by Alexandre Benois as part of her costume for a role in Stravinsky's ballet *Petrushka*. The dresser in the background is captured sewing, perhaps mending the dancer's dress. The print is based on the painting *Prima ballerina and dresser* (exhibited at the Alpine Club, London, 1922) but with the composition reversed. Knight's graphic work developed during the 1920s and in 1924 she was elected an Associate of the Royal Society of Painter-Etchers, becoming a full member in 1932. In the same year, Knight was the only woman to feature as Number 29 in the 32-volume *Modern Masters of Etching*, published between 1925 and 1932.[18]

From Knight's first visit to see the Ballets Russes on stage, her depictions of the ballet appeared regularly among her exhibited works. Her poster (Fig. 11) was designed to advertise Knight's 'Pictures of the Russian Ballet' exhibition, which opened at the Leicester Galleries on 23 June 1920. Ballerinas Pavlova and Tamara Karsavina both attended the opening, and to coincide with the exhibition, *The Times* newspaper published its first Women's Supplement with a special feature on Knight, alongside several of her pictures.

The following year, a portfolio '21 Drawings of Russian Ballet' (1921) was published, its contents mainly sketches of Karsavina, Lopokova and Léonide Massine, with the frontispiece showing 'Karsavina in the Three Cornered Hat'. In April 1922, the Alpine Club, London, held a solo exhibition of Knight's work. In the catalogue introduction by EV Lucas, the exhibition's wide-ranging subject matter was described: 'All artists are enviable in that their occupation is with beauty, but Knight is peculiarly so, in being free to divide her time in such an ideal way: in summer among the rocks and pools and moorlands of the Delectable Duchy, and in winter in the dressing room of Lydia Lopokova.'[19]

Knight's works *In the Coulisses* (Fig. 12) and *Carnaval* (Fig. 13) were both purchased from the Alpine Club's exhibition by their municipal owners. *In the Coulisses* she depicts a dress rehearsal at the Alhambra Theatre, London in 1919, capturing the dancers for the ballets *Les Sylphides* and *Le Tricorne*. The startling white tulle of the ballerina's dress is in contrast to their dresser, in vivid red, who stands in the wings to their right, on hand for any necessary dress adjustments.

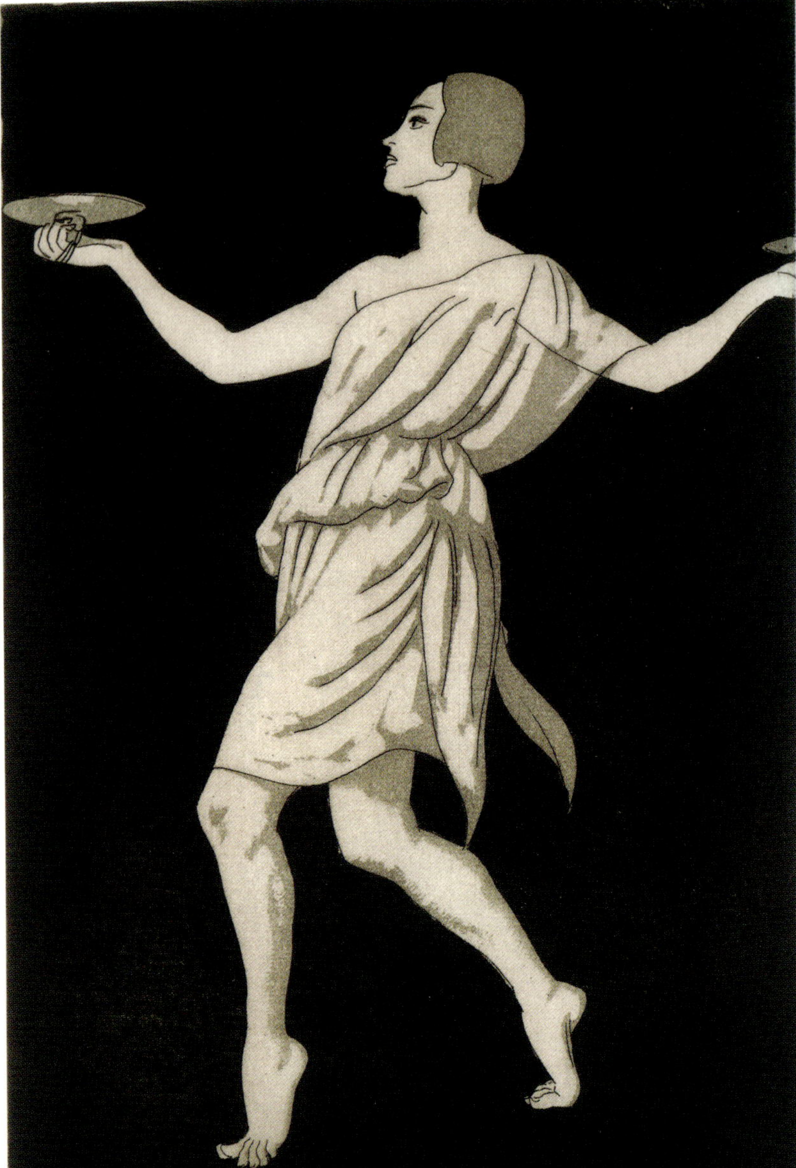

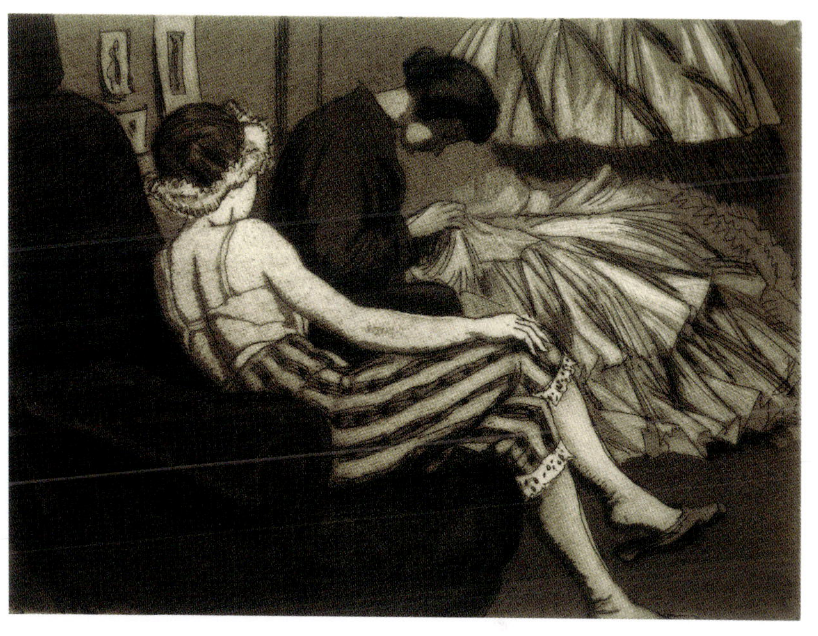

9. (opposite) *Grecian Dancer No.1 (Pavlova)*, 1923, etching and aquatint
10. (above) *Dressing Room No.1*, 1923, etching and aquatint

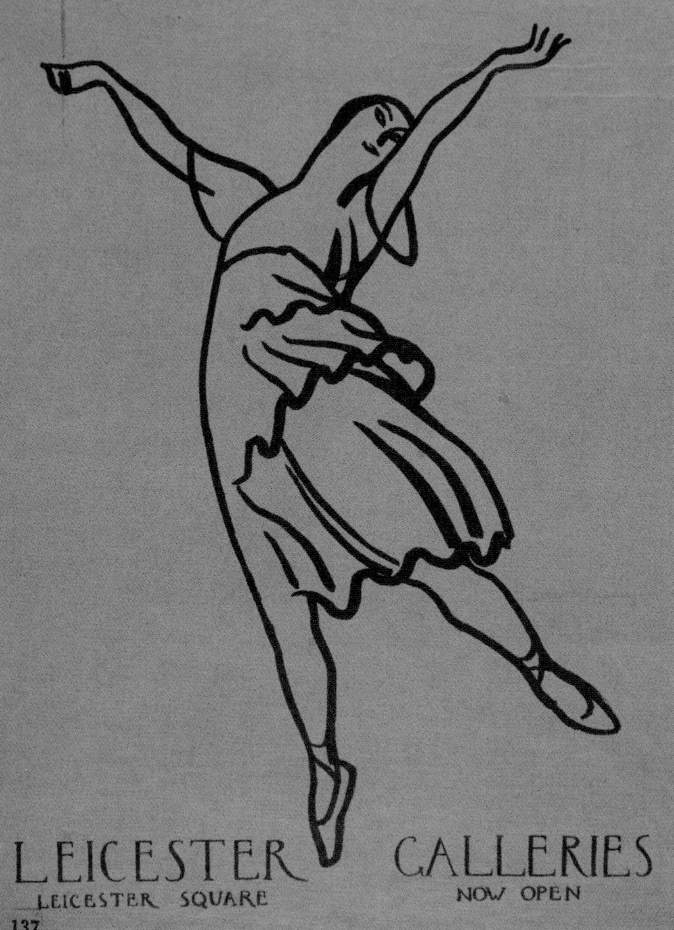

PICTURES & DRAWINGS OF
THE RUSSIAN BALLET
BY
LAURA KNIGHT
LEICESTER GALLERIES
LEICESTER SQUARE
NOW OPEN
137

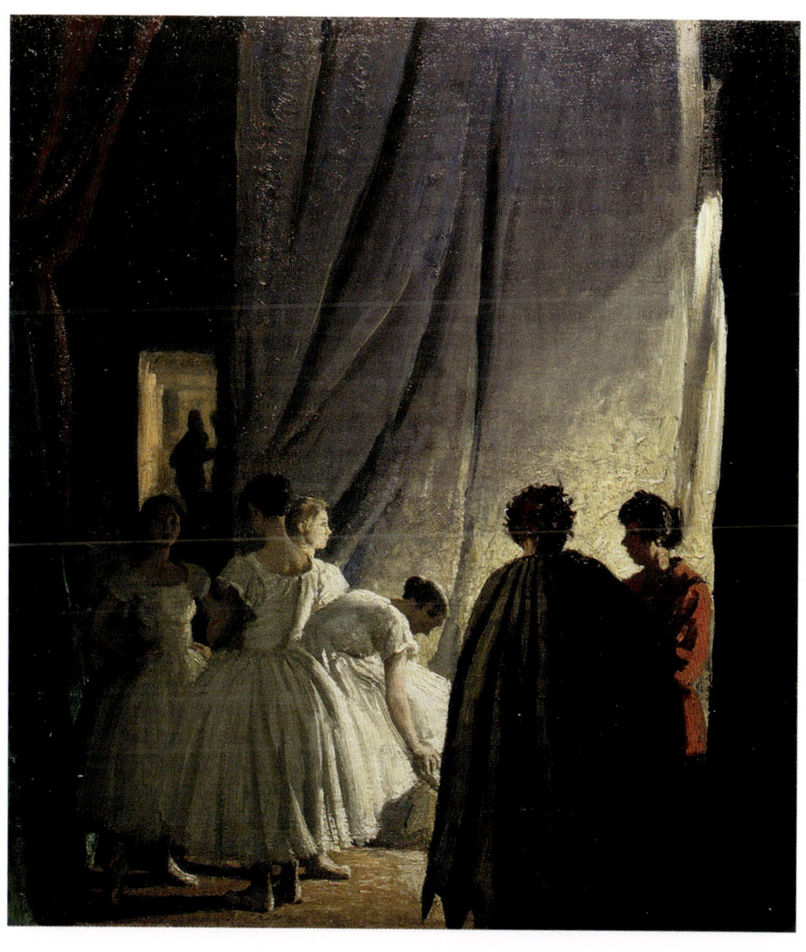

11. (opposite) Exhibition poster, 1920, lithograph
12. (above) *In the Coulisses – Behind the Scenes*, 1921, oil on panel

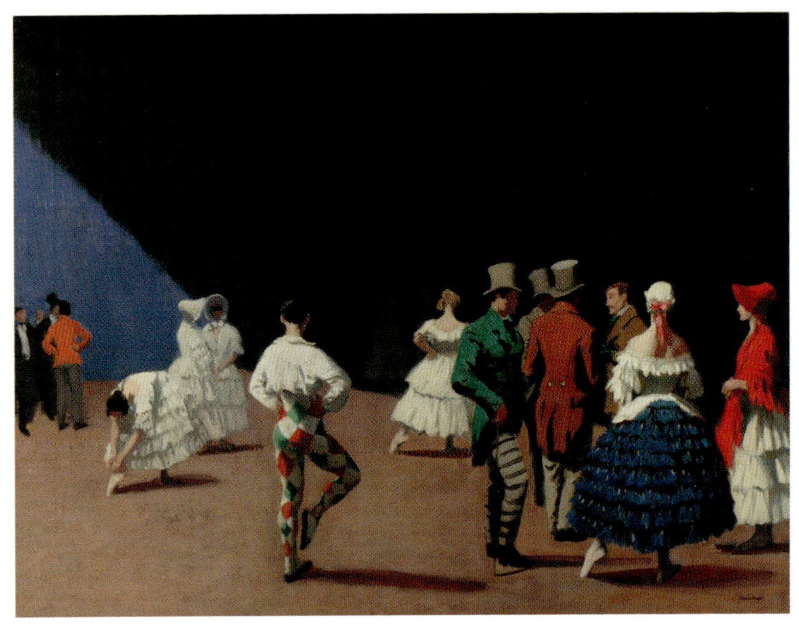

13. *Carnaval*, 1920, oil on canvas

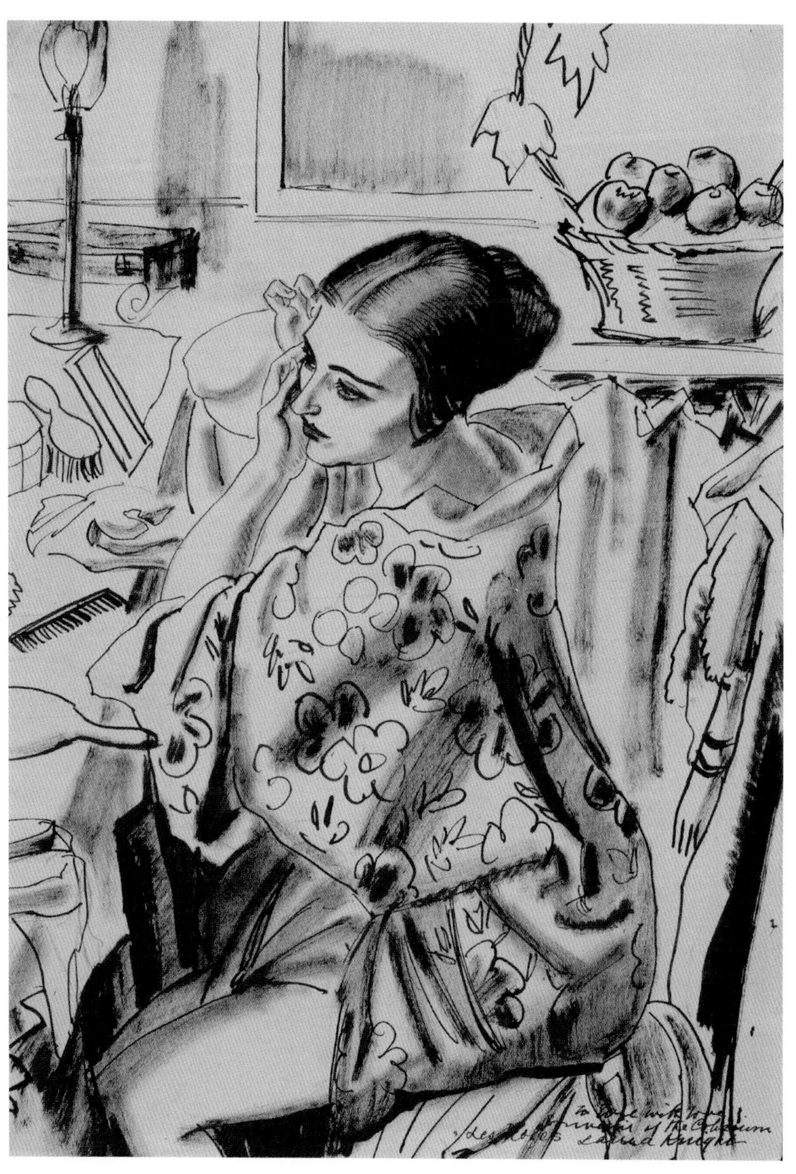

14. *Vanda Evina in Les Roses*, 1924, pen and ink

In *Carnaval*, Knight captures the lustrous colours and bold designs of Leon Bakst – the Russian designer who gained fame for the ballets he created for the Ballets Russes. Here Knight depicts dancers on the stage before curtain up; the jewel-like colours of their dresses set against the deep shadowed recesses of the wings in the background.

Knight's relationship with the Ballets Russes was further cemented in 1924 when she was commissioned to design the costumes for the ballet *Les Roses*. Her pen and ink portrait of the ballerina Vanda Evina in her dressing room at the Coliseum (Fig. 14), making herself up for her role in *Les Roses*, is inscribed 'To Evie with love. A souvenir of the Coliseum & "The Roses". Laura Knight.'

Circus Folk

The longing for the glittering lights, the smell of the grease paint and powder in the warm crowded air of the dressing room wagon, of the smell of the sawdust and the stables was what they were longing for. The fresh air of the tents, the adventure and change, the excitement of pulling out in front of the public and the applause. There is a saying in the circus that if you have one pair of shoes worn out tenting, you can never leave it permanently for anything else. Sooner or later, you will return.[20]

From the mid-1920s, Knight developed an interest in the circus life and between 1929 and 1930 she toured with Great Carmo's and Bertram Mills' circus (Fig. 15). In Knight's account of her travels she experienced both the exhilaration of the circus performances and the harsh reality of life on the road: 'No one outside could understand my happiness in the life we led. I did not mind discomfort if there was plenty of water for washing and Ally always bought good food … What was mere luxury compared to the joy of living right in the middle of my subject – the people, animals I knew!'[21]

Knight's working methods allowed her to portray her circus subject matter under often challenging circumstances. Over 300 of her accomplished drawings are in the RA Collection, including depictions of the big top tent under construction, acrobats and tight rope-walkers, as well as lions and horses.

The work *The Three Clowns* (Fig. 16) was exhibited in the RA's annual exhibition of 1930. The clown to the right was Knight's close friend Joe Bert, an acrobat and trapeze artist from Belfast. Nottinghamshire County's archives hold Knight's hand-typed reminiscences of this circus performer, which she used for *A Proper Circus Omie* (1962). This book is richly illustrated with 42 of her circus drawings and paintings and dedicated to the late Bert's wife Ally, a great friend of Knight's (Ally became Knight's companion and housekeeper).

'Although my interest in clowns was extra special,' explained Knight, 'it had a rival – horses. Never before had I had a chance of making a study of these marvellous creatures, but you can't paint circus life if you can't draw a horse.'[22] Knight would demonstrate her ability to portray the horse in November 1930, when her circus work culminated in the exhibition *Circus Folk*, arranged by Ernest Brown at the Alpine Club Gallery. Exhibited works included *The Rosinbacks* (Fig. 17), later acquired by City Museum and Art Gallery, Stoke on Trent. Bernard Darwin wrote in *Country Life* on 1 November 1930:

> Dame Knight Knight has recaptured for us the feeling of romance ... She has helped us to breathe once more the airs of our youth, the genuine sawdusty breezes which still blow across the heath ... she has depicted her circus folk gravely, without a touch of sentimentality or of levity – serious men and women, seriously earning their living in a skilful and difficult business; not unhappy nor outcast nor rakish nor in the least conscious of being romantic, just people ... getting on with their job.[23]

The V&A holds a 1935 etching of a version of the same image in its collection, entitled *Bareback Rider* (Fig. 18). A female

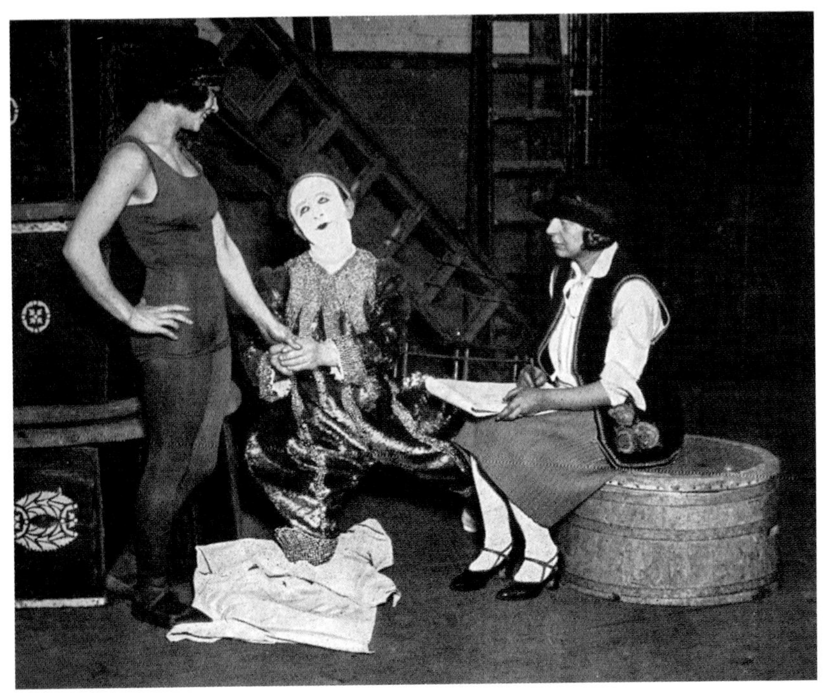

15. Laura Knight at the Circus, 1928

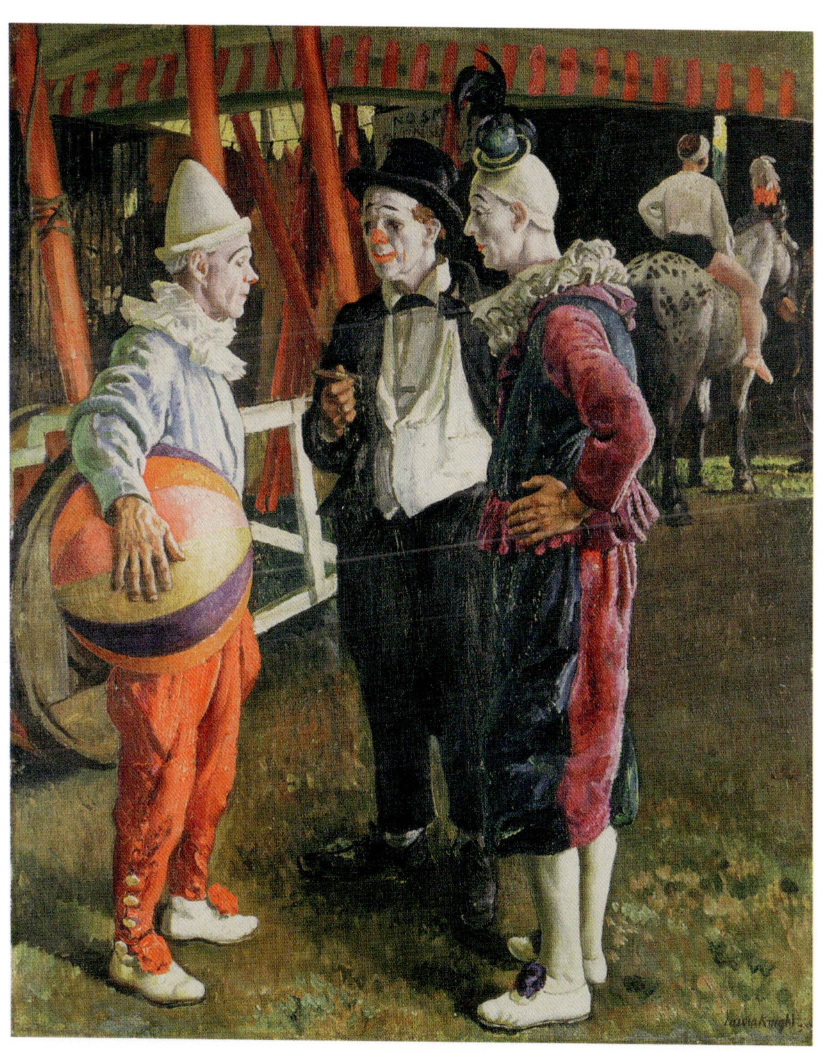

16. *The Three Clowns*, 1930, oil on canvas

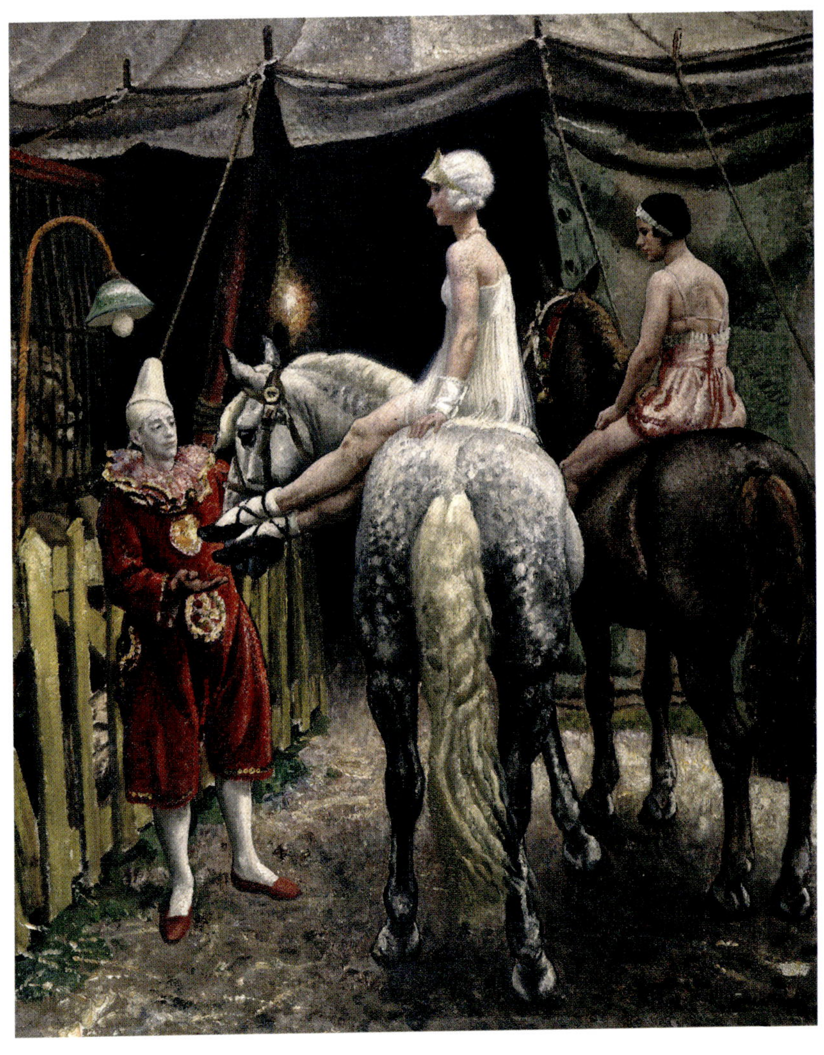

17. (above) *The Rosinbacks*, 1930, oil on canvas
18. (opposite) *Bareback Rider*, 1935, etching

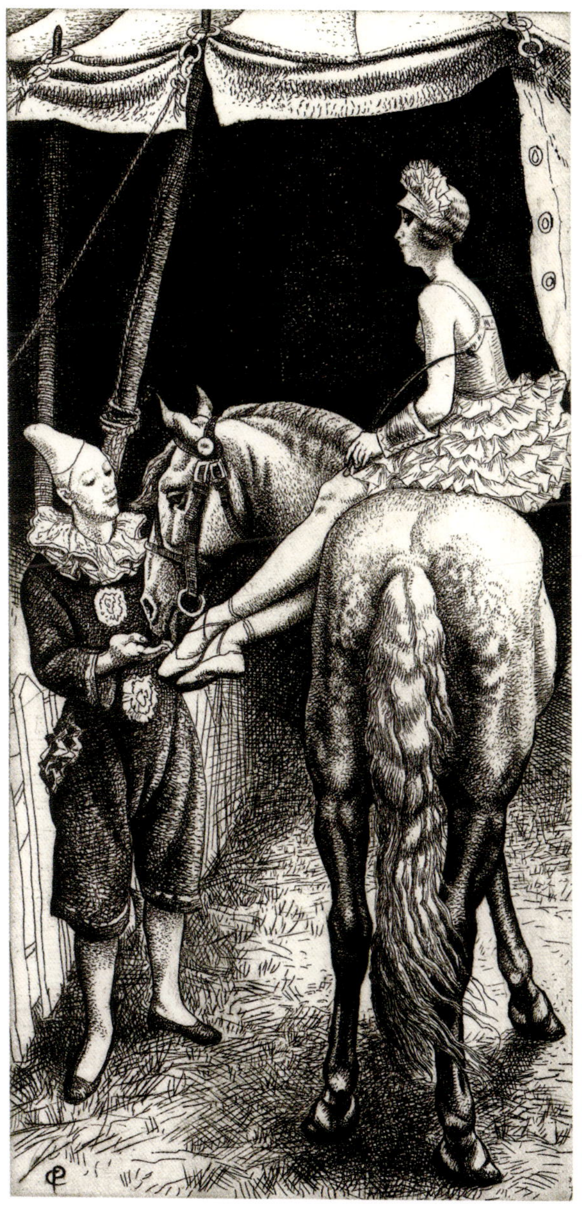

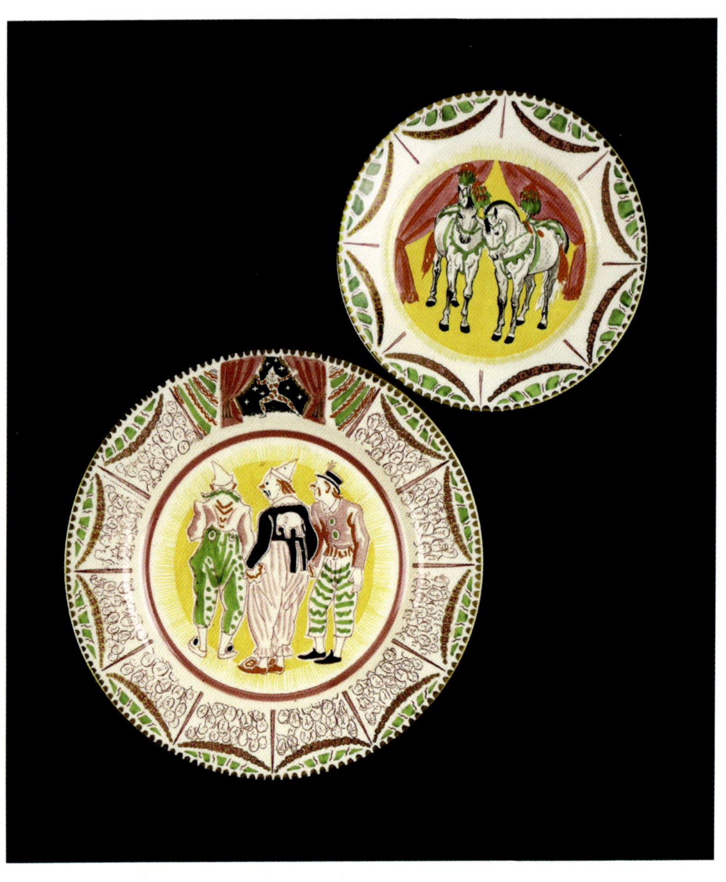

19. Two 'Bizarre' side plates from the 'Circus' series, depicting
two performing horses, and three clowns, 1934, ceramic

performer sits in her tulle tutu on the back of a dappled grey horse being held by her clown companion. Many of Knight's prints of the circus were used to illustrate her first autobiography *Oil Paint & Grease Paint*, and she also used her work from this period to collaborate with Royal Staffordshire Pottery. Her 'Circus' dinner service (Fig. 19) was designed by Knight in 1934 and manufactured by Arthur J. Wilkinson & Co Ltd at Royal Staffordshire Pottery under the direction of the ceramic artist Clarice Cliff. Knight's decorations transform the flat ceramic surface of a platter into a circus ring around with a cheering crowd, and each dinner plate depicts a different circus act, in which horses, lions, trapeze artists and brightly dressed clowns appear. Even the handles on each tureen are modelled as clowns.

The Gypsy Way of Life

Throughout the 1930s Knight was interested in capturing the gypsy way of life. In 1931, she first attended the Derby meeting on Epsom Downs, perhaps at Munnings' suggestion. She returned to Epsom every year throughout the 1930s and also visited the races at Ascot. During this period Knight produced over 60 gypsy-related canvases.

Following the acquaintances she made at the races with the gypsy community, Knight was subsequently invited to visit their camp on the common at Iver, Buckinghamshire. Over a two-year period she became fascinated by the way the gypsies lived the travelling life in their traditional painted wagons (Fig. 20).

The relaxed pose of Knight's gypsy sitters is evident in *The Gypsy* (Fig. 21). Completed inside the sitter's wagon, the outline of a brass bed behind him, the work shows the speed at which Knight worked to depict her gypsy subjects. The paint is thinly applied in areas of the canvas, but the facial features and the loosely tied scarf around the gypsy's neck are rendered in detail. This work was purchased for the Tate Gallery as part of the Chantrey Bequest.

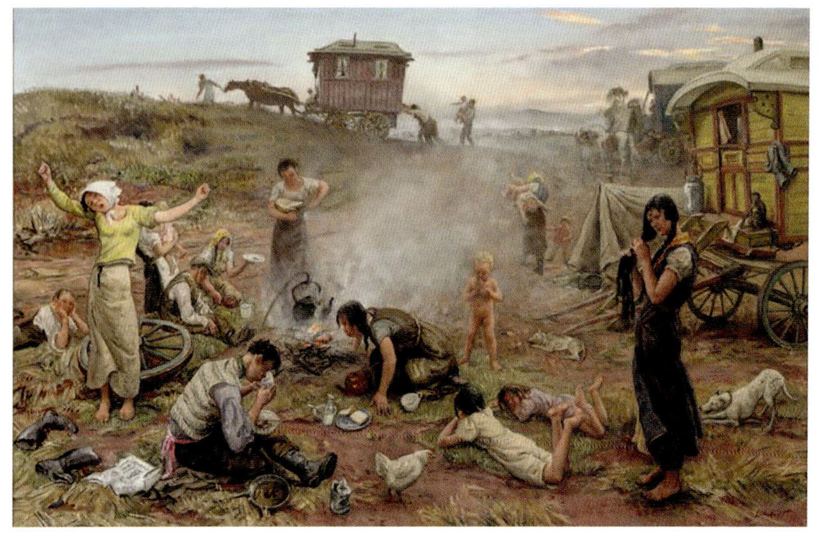

20. (above) *Early Morning at a Gypsy Camp*, n.d, oil on canvas
21. (opposite) *The Gypsy*, exhibited 1939, oil on canvas

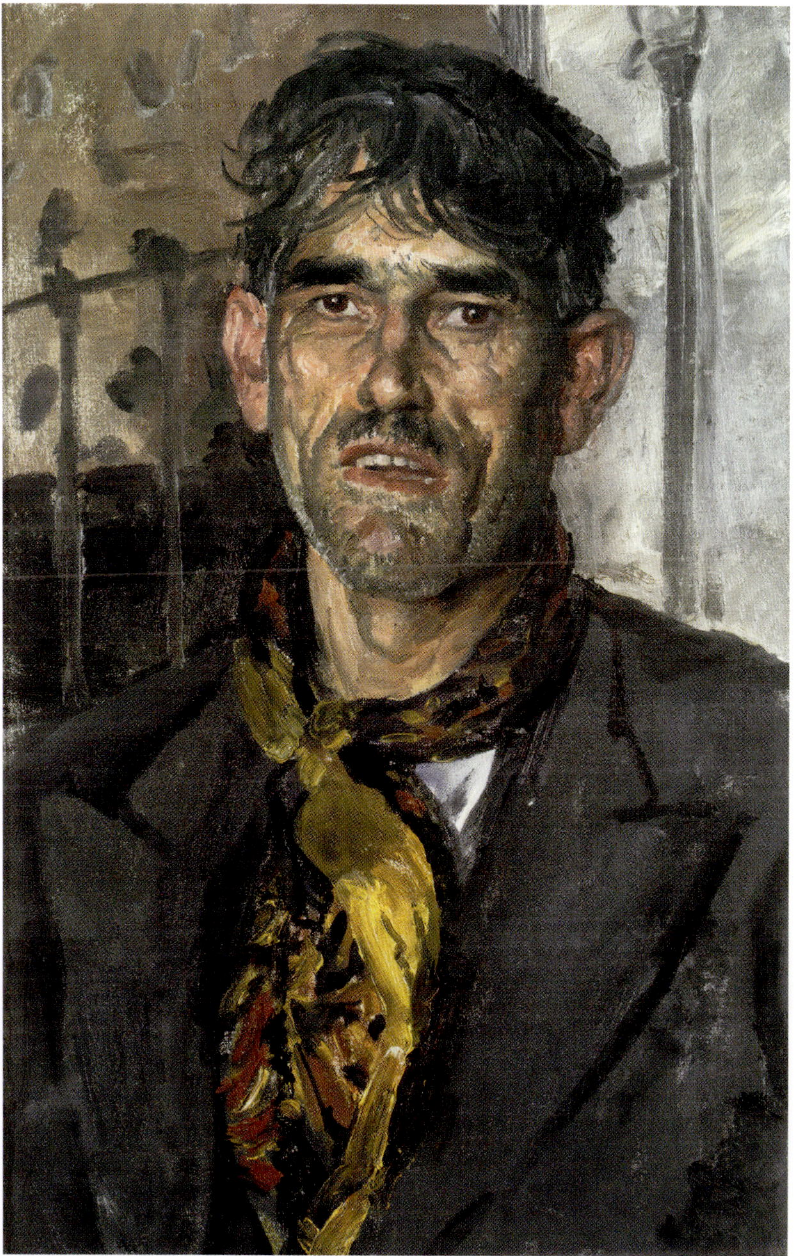

Knight wrote of this period: 'It was one of the most inspiring times of my working life. An immense wild rose-bush, gaudy with bloom, that flourished on the common, typified the gypsy in its freedom of bloom and thorn. I was at home with these people – found them kindly and willing to pose . . .'[24]

Second World War Commissions

During the Second World War, the role of providing a pictorial war record led to the formation of the War Artists' Advisory Committee (WAAC) in November 1939, as part of the British Ministry of Information. The WAAC sought to assemble a collection of works that recorded life at the Front, and in wartime Britain too. The Committee commissioned more than 300 artists to depict the war, of which 48 were women. These artists focused mainly on female contributions to the war effort. Seventeen of Knight's war works were acquired by the WAAC; only Evelyn Dunbar and Ethel Gabain surpassed the amount of Knight's acquired works, with 40 and 38 works respectively.[25]

In 1939, Knight was approached by the government regarding a poster commission for a series on 'Britain's War Effort', which would depict food production. A poster design was commissioned to highlight the work of the Women's Land Army (WLA). Knight was offered a sum of 10 guineas for a preparatory sketch, and 70 guineas for the finished work. Knight accepted the commission but objected to the stipulation requiring her to submit a sketch. The secretary of the WAAC insisted that this was necessary, even in the case of a distinguished artist such as herself; Knight reluctantly accepted the conditions and after many delays, due to the 'terrible British weather', studied members of the WLA at work in the fields of Malvern.[26]

The WAAC rejected Knight's first submission on the basis that 'the emphasis in your design is so very strongly on the horses and so little on the girl that the message which we wish to convey would not really get to the public'.[27] She changed

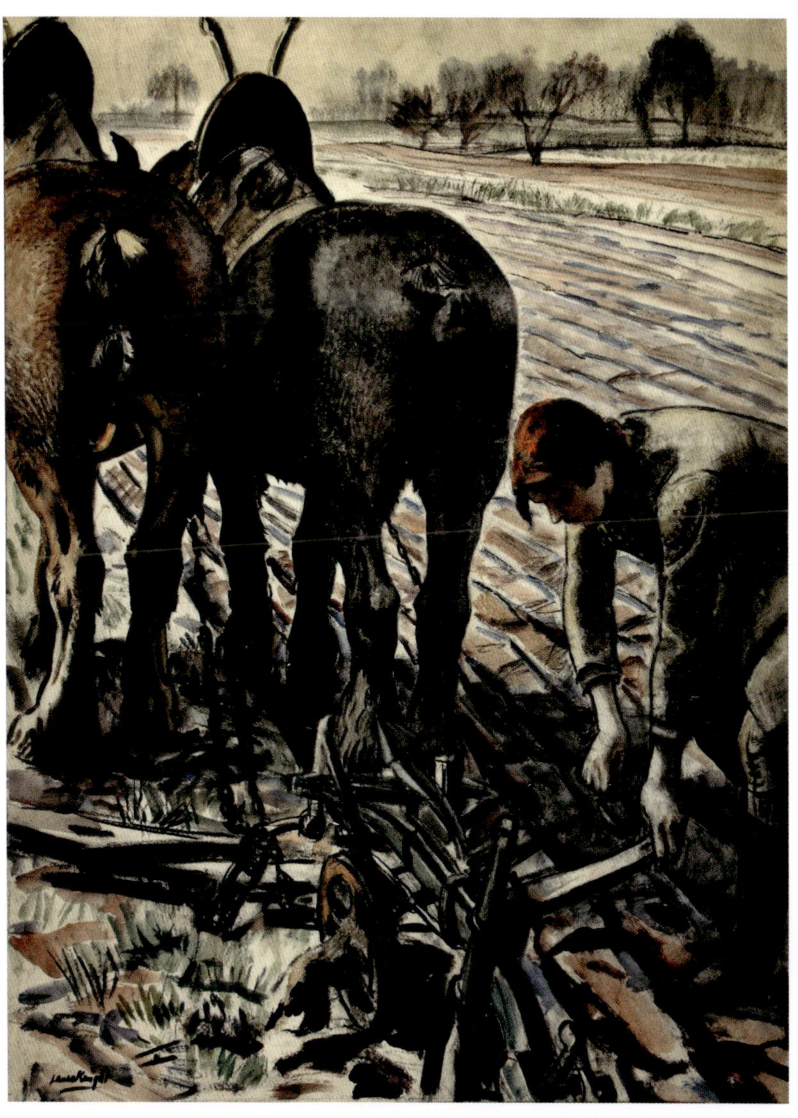

22. *Land Army Girl*, c.1944, charcoal, pencil and watercolour on board

the illustration from three girls working a plough, to just one girl as seen in *Land Army Girl* (Fig. 22). This final design was submitted and accepted by the government for the poster.

Following Knight's poster commission, in January 1940, she was asked by the WAAC to go to London to paint scenes after an air raid. She replied by return of post: 'I regret I shall be unable to accept the fee, 50 guineas, and £1-0-0 per day expenses for painting the air raids and shelters. I understand that Artists are asked to take less than their usual fees, but I do not see that such a sum would cover the expenses of living and canvases.'[28] Despite Knight's rejection, later that year she was asked by the WAAC to portray a distinguished member of the Women's Auxiliary Air Force (WAAF).

In August 1940, Knight agreed to paint a head and shoulders portrait of a WAAF officer, for a fee of 35 guineas, if the officer would come to Malvern. The subject of the painting was a heroine of the war, Daphne Pearson (Fig. 23). During an air raid on 31 May 1940, Pearson was outside the WAAF buildings in Detling, Kent. A friendly bomber crashed close by her on take-off, and despite knowing there were unexploded bombs on the aircraft, Corporal Pearson rushed to the wreckage rescuing the pilot and protecting him from the bomb blast. She was award-ed an Empire Gallantry Medal, later transmuted into a George Cross, becoming the first woman recipient of the medal.

Knight portrays her subject looking up at the sky and carrying a respirator. Originally Knight presented the portrait showing Corporal Pearson holding a rifle. Falling foul of the censors, women at this time were not permitted to bear arms, and so the rifle had to be painted out in favour of a gas mask.

The portrait of Corporal Pearson was considered a great success by the WAAC, and Knight was then asked to paint a composite picture of the first three members of the WAAF to be awarded military medals: Corporal Robins, Assistant Section

23. *Corporal JDM Pearson, GC, WAAF*, 1940, oil on canvas

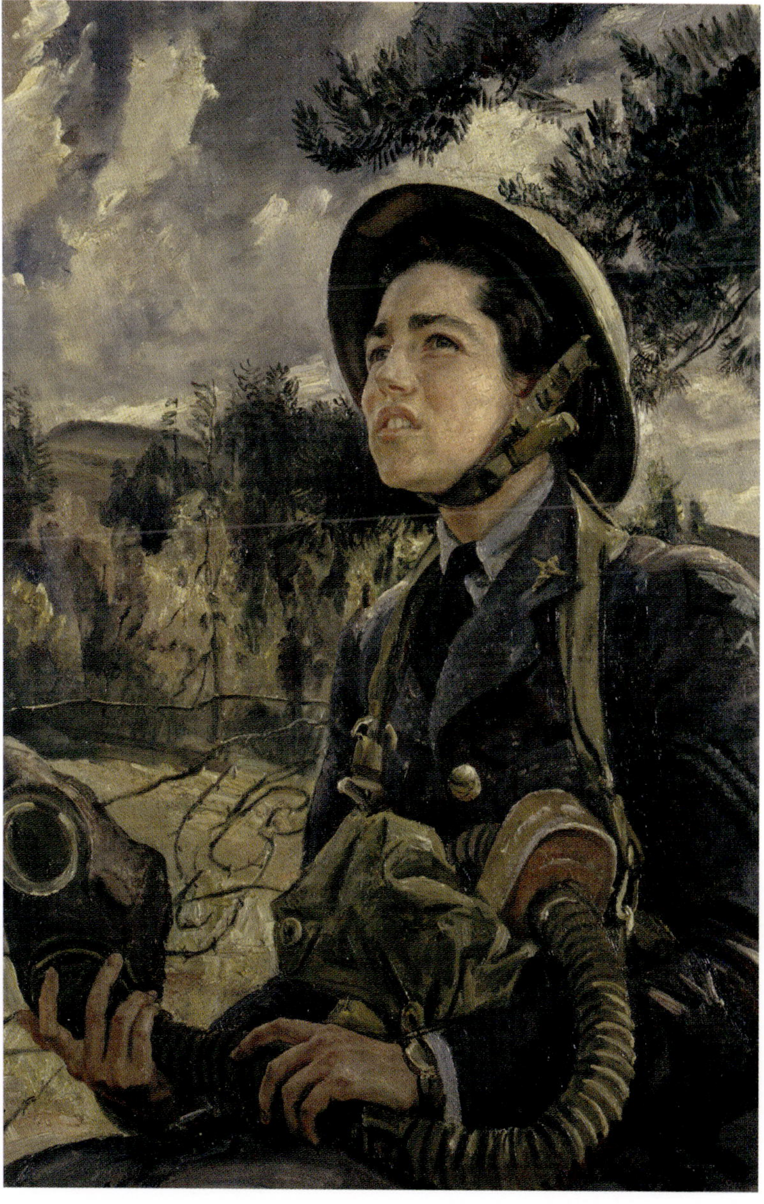

Leader Henderson and Sergeant Turner. Knight was offered a fee of 60 guineas, which she at once rejected. The WAAC wrote: 'The Committee sympathize with your point that it was at least as difficult to paint a group of three sitters as to paint three separate portraits and they have now recommended that you should receive a fee of 35 guineas for each portrait.'[29] The original commission was replaced in favour of a joint portrait of Henderson and Turner and a separate portrait of Corporal Robins.

Following the success of Knight's portraits of servicewomen, the WAAC commissioned her to portray the vital work of women working with barrage balloons. Initially used during the First World War, barrage balloons were an integral part of Britain's defences during the Second World War, and by September 1941, 2,748 barrage balloons were in use. Knight was invited by the Air Ministry to paint WAAF balloon fabric workers employed in the inspection and maintenance of barrage balloons. She wrote to the WAAC:

> I have not heard what my remuneration for this work is likely to be, but trust that the offer will be on a more generous scale than for portraits. The work entailed a monetary loss for me. Much as I enjoy doing this work, I shall find it difficult to continue [painting] more at such a fee, considering so much now goes in Income Tax. I should love to do this work and I do hope you will seriously consider what I have just told you.[30]

She received a replying saying that the remuneration was not the concern of the WAAC and it would be for the Air Ministry to arrange her fees. The letter added that the Committee had recently decided that the standard fees for portraits should be raised to 50 guineas for a head and shoulders or 75 guineas for a half-length. Perhaps Knight's persistence over raising fees had gone some way to achieving an increase.

Knight was finally offered 100 guineas for her barrage balloon commission; she accepted the offer and went to a WAAF camp near Sheffield in 1942. As a centre of steel manufacture, Sheffield was a target for bombing raids and barrage balloons were used as a key defence of the city. Knight's work *In for Repairs* (Fig. 24) depicts a partially inflated barrage balloon being repaired. Knight later wrote to the officer commanding the barrage balloons in Sheffield: 'The balloon posed like a great silver toad with a pulse in its side, due I suppose to the draught coming in from the door.'[31] *In for Repairs* so impressed the Air Ministry representative that he persuaded the WAAC to commission *A Balloon Site, Coventry* (Fig. 25) for help in recruiting 'just the right sort of person for this particular class of work'.[32]

This work depicts the coordinated skills of the balloon crew in operation at Spencer Park in Coventry. The barrage balloon is being hoisted into position by WAAF women in blue overalls, with the industrial city of Coventry visible in the background. In Knight's introduction to *War Pictures by British Artists: Women* (1943) written the year after this painting was completed, she writes of the women she met working on the barrage balloons:

> Come fine, come storm, by day or night, the Balloon must go up or down, be tended as a living thing, a guardian. The occasion may be a mere point's change in the wind: her wings deflate, flap and inflate; unwieldy, she dips her monstrous bulk as the 'hands' manoeuvre her ... Last night a half-gale sprang up; to-day the Balloon is storm-bedded; the lashings, a network on its sides; press as into the flesh of a colossal silver toad. In snow and gale these girls do their duty ... No praise is too high for their staunchness, be they in crowded districts, or in lonely places miles from home – and from the cinema.[33]

The WAAC devoted considerable attention to commissioning artists to portray the munitions and armament industries, and those employed in them. Approximately one third of the total output in British factories during the Second World War was made possible by the 5.5 million women working in production.

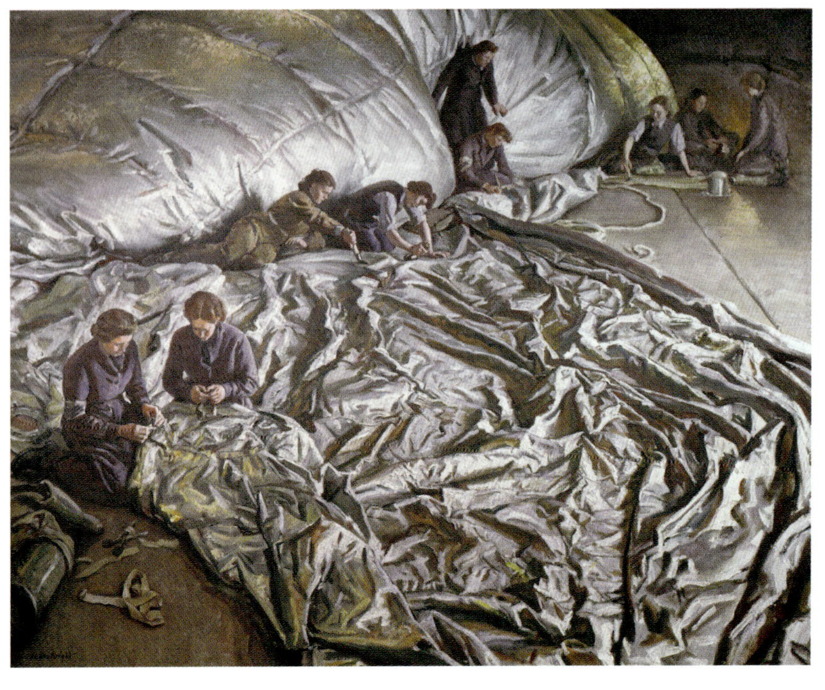

24. *In for Repairs*, 1942, oil on canvas

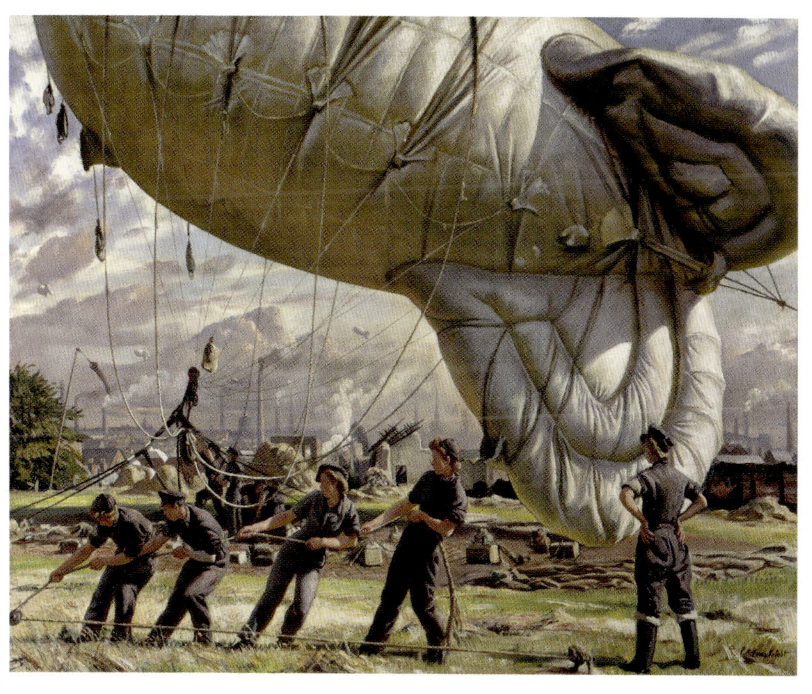

25. *A Balloon Site, Coventry*, 1943, oil on canvas

Towards the end of 1942, Knight was asked to paint Ruby Loftus, an Royal Ordnance Factory worker who undertook one of the most difficult operations in the making of armaments – screwing the breech ring for a Bofors gun (Fig. 26). Failure to complete this procedure correctly could result in a violent blow-back when the gun was fired.

In March 1943, Knight agreed to a fee of 100 guineas and expenses following what was now a customary wrangle between her and the WAAC regarding her fees and place of work. Her astuteness in recognising the value of her work was demonstrated through her negotiating skills with the WAAC and insistence of fair remuneration. Later that month she travelled to the Newport Ordnance Factory and stayed in a house belonging to the factory. On her first morning at the factory she arrived with her canvas, charcoal and paints. While Loftus continued working, Knight set up her easel and a temporary low partition guarded her from passing workers.

Ruby Loftus recalled: 'Dame Knight watched me working for a day, making rough sketches of me all the time. Then at the end of the day she decided which one she liked best, which was one full of "GO" as she put it.'[34] Knight described sketching Ruby at the factory:

> It would seem that the grim necessities of this war have even further enlarged their opportunities in spheres formerly considered foreign to their sex. For instance, the engineering shop ... among the operators of big machine tools, is a young creature bent over a lathe. The suds fly from the great wheel, which is like a Catherine-wheel in a firework display; filings curl in long strands ... as with intent look she gauges the depth of the cutting.[35]

The painting was first shown at the RA's 1943 annual exhibition and subsequently voted Picture of the Year. Loftus' story and portrait were also included as 'ROF Girl's Portrait is Picture of the Year' in a British Paramount News short film (*War Work News No 22*), which showed Knight, Ruby and Sir Charles McLaren

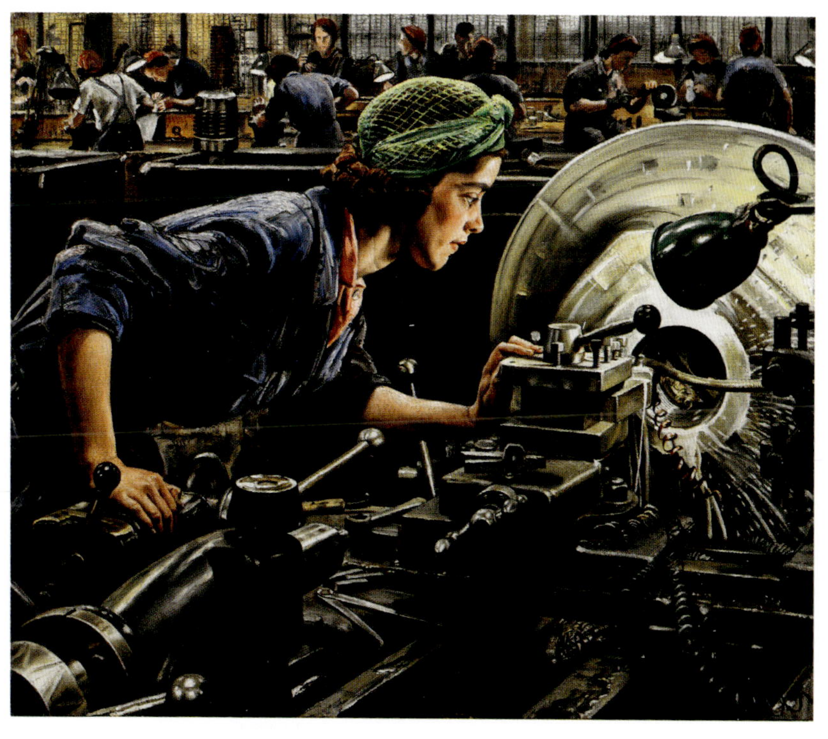

26. *Ruby Loftus Screwing a Breech-Ring*, 1943, oil on canvas

Director-General of the Royal Ordnance Factories inspecting the painting at the RA, followed by footage of Ruby carrying out the operation.

During the same year, *War Pictures by British Artists: Women* was published as part of the title's second series. Knight was asked to write the introduction; in her text, she stated that pictures of women's activities in wartime:

> ... with many others, will have their place side by side with those of sailors, soldiers and the airmen, when the artists' record of the war is complete. After what she has done in this titanic struggle, will she not guard what she has gained, and to Man's effort add her own? If she can do what she has done in war, what may she not do in peace?[36]

Election to the Royal Academy

> One of the greatest moments of Mother's life came when she found that I, a mere baby, was never so content as with pencil and paper; even before I could speak or walk I drew. There was no question of my purpose in life. I remember her saying when I was only a few years old, 'You will be elected to the Royal Academy one day'.[37]

In 1927, at the age of 50, Knight was elected an Associate of the Royal Academy (ARA), becoming only the second woman ARA since its foundation in 1768. Annie Swynnerton had been elected ARA five years earlier, in 1922, but her standing was not followed by the promotion of other women into the RA's ranks. Swynnerton was the only ARA between 1922 and 1927, and of the four other women elected ARAs between 1927 and 1948 – Knight, Procter, Ethel Walker in 1940 and Margaret Fisher Prout in 1948 – only the first two were promoted to full RAs.

To be eligible for nomination as an ARA, painters (the nomination process was slightly different for sculptors, architects

and engravers) needed to be nominated by at least five members. Once those signatures had been collected, the painter's
name appeared on the list of candidates for nomination each
time a new ARA was to be elected. If the nominee had still not
been elected within seven years, their name was removed from
the list and the process had to start again.

Knight was first nominated in 1915 but still had not been
elected by 1922, when she had to be nominated again. Three
artists, George Clausen, William Lionel Wyllie and Julius Olsson,
nominated Knight in both cases. She was one of two ARAs
elected on 1 November 1927 along with Francis Dodd. Dodd was
elected first, gaining one vote more than Knight before she
was comfortably elected ahead of RG Eves.

Interestingly, even after her nomination in 1915, no votes
were cast in favour of her election until 1923, by which time
Swynnerton had become the first female ARA. In 1923, Knight
twice received three votes and the occasional vote over the
next few years, before suddenly receiving great support in 1927.
There were two elections of ARAs in 1927; in the first election
on 21 April 1927 she received no votes. The sudden surge of
support for Knight in 1927 is interesting: why does her nomination come about now? Some artists consistently appear in the
election minutes, receiving more and more votes, their even-
tual election coming to seem inevitable. Knight, on the other
hand, came pretty much out of nowhere, having been on the
list for 12 years.[38] Following her election 'an army of pressmen
and photographers' camped outside her studio, emphasising
her rags-to-riches story and she also featured in a British Pathé
newsreel.[39] Her election was also marked by a commission from
one of the leading society photographers, Alexander Bassano,
in which she adopts a variety of guises.[40]

Other women artists considered for ARA around the same
time as Knight include Anna Airy, nominated in 1919, Henrietta
Rae, nominated in 1920 and Lucy Kemp-Welch, nominated in
1920. Kemp-Welch received votes before Knight, and in 1921–2

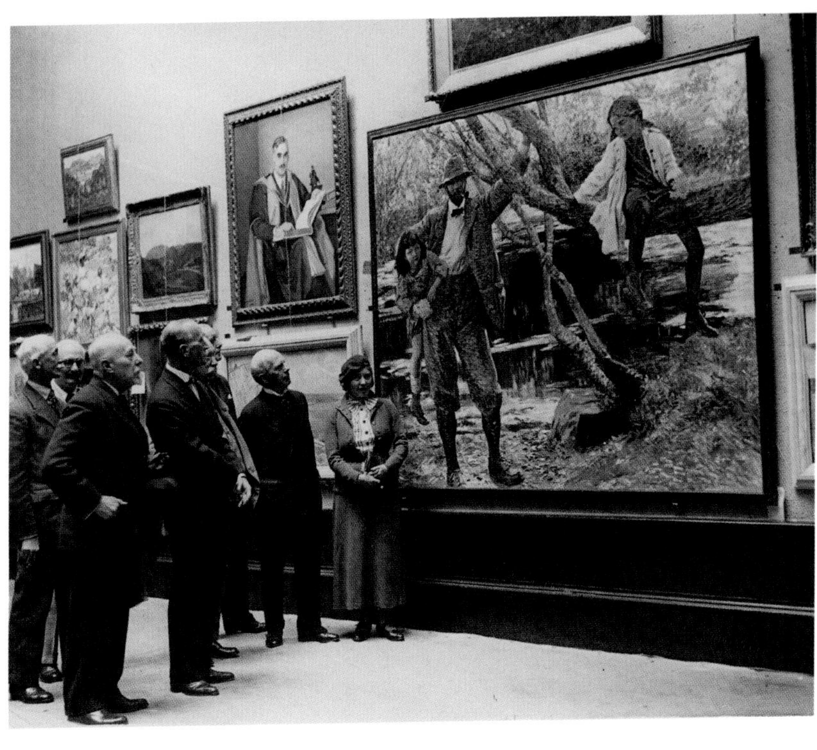

27. Laura Knight at the 166th Royal Academy Summer Exhibition, 1934

it would have seemed that she was more likely to become an Academician than Knight. It is interesting to consider why Swynnerton and Knight were elected, and not the others. Indeed, the limited number of women elected to the RA is not representative of the number of women artists who exhibited regularly at the RA during this period. In fact, the pool of prospective professional women candidates for possible election to the RA was considerably larger than the small number actually elected would indicate (Fig. 27).

In 1936, Knight was elevated to Royal Academician, the first woman to be a full Academician since its foundation. As a full Academician, Knight participated in the selection and hanging of the annual exhibition. On her election, a special law had to be passed to enable Knight to become a member of the Council because of her gender.[41] She served on the Council for two years, describing the proceedings in some detail in her 1965 autobiography *The Magic of a Line*. Knight comments that her friend Procter 'never availed herself of the privilege of admittance to the more intimate concerns of that institution,' instead spending summers in Newlyn and winters in the West Indies.[42]

The year after her election, Knight became the first woman artist to sit on the hanging committee for the Summer Exhibition at the RA. She was also on the hanging committee in 1946 – the only woman artist to sit on the exhibition panel in the first half of the twentieth century. However, that women were present at all could be construed as a token gesture: Knight's gender prevented her from attending the RA's all-male annual banquet (women RAs and ARAs were barred from attending until 1967). Only after campaigning by Gertrude Hermes, elected an ARA in 1963, were women finally included in the RA annual banquet. Maxwell Fry recalled how 'the spirit of truth and justice' overwhelmed him as he watched Knight slowly descending the RA staircase. 'She has been a member much longer than me', Hermes told him, 'but never a dinner has she eaten in this place.'[43]

In 1965, the RA honoured Knight with a large retrospective exhibition in the Diploma Galleries, the sixth living artist to be so honoured and the first woman Royal Academician (a further 20 years would elapse before another woman RA, Elisabeth Frink, would be recognised with a retrospective at the Academy in 1985). Works were drawn from throughout Knight's career, and from a wide range of private and public collections. Knight's unceasing work ethic at the age of 88 is captured in an illustrated letter to Ella and Charles Naper written during the hanging of the 1965 exhibition:

> I have just come back from the R.A. where I have spending [*sic*] a day cataloguing and such like. The beautifully refurbished Diploma Galleries – four of them, are filled with more than 250 works, oils, watercolours, drawings and etchings by L.K. A gorgeous background that is very pleasing. What I want to tell you particularly is that both of you are there – not as large as life – but I hope twice as natural. The old 'Spring' picture has been yanked out of the Tate. Age has not wrinkled either the paint or yourselves.[44]

A reviewer of the exhibition in *The Times* wrote that whilst 'sheltered' from Modernism, 'few women artists have delved so widely in the curiosities of life around them and painted what they saw with each observant and transparent delight.'[45] As a keen chronicler of early twentieth-century life in Britain, regardless of her gender, Knight's work allows us to enjoy and observe ways of living that have largely disappeared from view. Her work may not be considered modern, in the sense that she didn't engage with the prevailing 'isms' of her time, but she captured the modern world and its inhabitants for us to enjoy today.

'A hard-working woman'

I am thankful to have known the tasks and struggles of
common life, joy and despair like any other mortal. I am just
a hard-working woman who longs to pierce the mystery of form
and colour.[46]

Widely celebrated during her lifetime for highlighting people's
working lives, Knight's work fell out of fashion after her death.
Her oeuvre was often criticised for employing an academic
model of representation that lacked subtlety in colour arrange-
ments and relied on camera-like compositions. Yet despite
being dismissed by Modernists for her lack of interest in formal
experiment, Knight's insistent realism made her one of the most
popular artists of the time. The current renewal of interest in
her work today, in exhibitions and through the art market, is
part of a wider resurgence of interest in British women artists.
The movement to address the imbalance in women artists' lack
of representation in public collections and on display in exhibitions now seeks to generate further interest in the work of these
artists. Once this disparity is addressed, their work, in particular
Knight's, will be restored to the cultural landscape and artistic
history of modern Britain.

Three days before a large retrospective exhibition at Nottingham Castle Museum and Art Gallery, Knight died aged 92 on
7 July 1970 at Langford Place, London. Her life 'lived spectacu-
larly, excitingly, dangerously, has formed the vivid patterns of
her work ... dancers, clowns, gypsies, the spangled girls of the
sawdust ring have been her models.'[47]

Notes

1 Laura Knight, *The Magic of a Line: The Autobiography of Laura Knight* (London 1965), p.368.

2 Laura Knight, *Oil Paint & Grease Paint* (London 1936), p.45.

3 Laura Knight, 'Can Women Succeed as Artists?', *Studio*, May 1922.

4 *The Manchester Guardian*, 12 Oct 1933.

5 EHG, 'Some Draw!', *Illustrated London News*, 21 Mar 1936, issue 5057, p.492.

6 Knight (cited note 2), p.162.

7 Ibid., p.179.

8 Herbert Thomas, 'Show Day at Newlyn', *The Cornish Telegraph*, 26 Mar 1914, p.3.

9 Anon., *The Times*, 16 Apr 1914, p.6.

10 Elected the first female Associate Member of the RA in 1922.

11 Claude Phillips, *The Daily Telegraph*, 17 Apr 1914, nb.

12 Letter dated 15 Nov 1957, Tate Archives.

13 This oil painting can be seen in the Front Hall of the RA, London.

14 Knight (cited note 1), p.154–7.

15 Knight (cited note 2), p.196.

16 Ibid., p.270.

17 Ibid., p.226.

18 Other artists to feature in the series included James McNeill Whistler, CRW Nevinson and Knight's friend William Russell Flint.

19 Catalogue for the Alpine Club exhibition, Apr 1920.

20 Knight (cited note 1), p.92.

21 Knight (cited note 2), p.347.

22 Knight (cited note 1), p.239.

23 Bernard Darwin, *Country Life*, 1 Nov 1930, p.43.

24 Knight (cited note 1), p.252.

25 17 of Stella Schmolle's works were also acquired, but as an independent submission rather than under commission.

26 Knight (cited note 1), p.277.

27 Laura Knight file, GP/55/74, Imperial War Museum.

28 Ibid.

29 Ibid.

30 Ibid.

31 Ibid.

32 Ibid.

33 Laura Knight, *War Pictures by British Artists: Women* (London 1943), p.7.

34 Ruby Loftus, *The Story of the Picture*, unpublished letter, Oct 1943.

35 Knight (cited note 33), p.10.

36 Ibid., p.56. Other booklets included *Soldiers,* with an introduction by William Coldstream, and *Production*, introduced by Cecil Beaton.

37 Knight (cited note 2), p.1.

38 Information regarding Knight's nomination as ARA and RA was kindly provided by James Finch, Curatorial Assistant, Royal Academy of Arts.

39 Knight (cited note 2), p.297.

40 See images NPG x19409–NPG x19414 and NPG x85440–NPG x85442, National Portrait Gallery, London.

41 Sidney C. Hutchison, *The History of the Royal Academy 1768–1986* (London 1986), p.161.

42 Knight (cited note 2), p.306.

43 Quoted in Jane Hill, *The Sculpture of Gertrude Hermes* (London 2011), p.69.

44 Letter from Laura Knight, 10 Jun 1965, now in the Estate of Ella Naper (see www.davidlay.co.uk/news-and-views/the-laura-knight-letters – last accessed 2 Jan 2019).

45 '74 years of Dame Knight', *The Times*, 17 Jul 1965.

46 Knight (cited note 2), p.391.

47 Stuart Fletcher, 'Number One Woman Artist', *Illustrated* magazine, 29 Jul 1939, p.39.

Appeal for information

I would like to appeal to all collectors, admirers and those commercially involved with the works of both Laura Knight and also her husband Harold Knight, to assist me in compiling a Catalogue Raisonné on the artists by:

1 Providing me with images and information to enable the Catalogue to become the recognised worldwide authority on the artists' lives and works.

2 Providing documented or supportable evidence such as correspondence, invoices or other written records to corroborate events and dates within the artists' lives, and to remove some current doubts and possible wrong assumptions that may have erroneously arisen to date.

R. John Croft FCA, Great nephew of Dame Laura Knight
Chairman – Trustees of the estate of Dame Laura Knight DBE RA RWS
PO Box 4710, Worthing, West Sussex, BN11 9JE
Email: info@damelauraknight.com
Website: www.damelauraknight.com

Image credits

Cover: *Assistant Section Leader E. Henderson, MM, and Sergeant H. Turner, MM, Women's Auxiliary Air Service*, 1941, oil on canvas, 114 × 81 cm, The Royal United Services Institute for Defence and Security Studies (gift from the War Artists' Advisory Committee, 1947). Photo © The Royal United Services Institute for Defence and Security Studies/ArtUK.

1. Madame Yevonde, photograph of Dame Laura Knight, 1967. Mary Evans / © Yevonde Portrait Archive.
2. *The Beach*, c.1909, oil on canvas, 127.6 × 153.2 cm, Laing Art Gallery, Newcastle-upon-Tyne, UK (purchased from HW Brooks, 1919). Photograph © Tyne & Wear Archives & Museums/Bridgeman Images.
3. *The Model* or *Laura Knight with model, Ella Louise Naper ('Self Portrait')*, 1913, oil on canvas 152.4 × 127.6 cm, National Portrait Gallery, London. Photograph © National Portrait Gallery, London.
4. *Two Dancers*, 1915, oil on enamel, 45 × 45 cm, Penlee House Gallery and Museum, Penzance. Photograph © Penlee House Gallery & Museum.
5. *The Cornish Coast*, 1917, oil on canvas, 64.8 × 76.3 cm. National Museum Wales, National Museum Cardiff, bequeathed by FH Lambert, 1940. Photograph courtesy National Museum of Wales.
6. *Spring*, 1916–19, oil on canvas, 152.4 × 182.9 cm. Tate, Presented by the Trustees of the Chantrey Bequest 1935 © Tate, London 2019.
7. *Physical Training at Witley Camp*, c.1917, oil on canvas, 304.8 × 365.7 cm, Canadian War Museum, Beaverbrook Collection of War Art [CWM19710261-0808]. Photograph courtesy Canadian War Museum.
8. *Les Sylphides*, 1919, oil on canvas, 76.2 x 101.6 cm, Birmingham Museums Trust, presented by Hugh L. Agnew, 1931. © Birmingham Museums Trust.
9. *Grecian Dancer No.1 (Pavlova)*, 1923, etching and aquatint, 24.9 × 17.5 cm, private collection. Photograph: © The Fine Art Society.
10. *Dressing Room No.1*, 1923, etching and aquatint, 14.9 × 19.8 cm, private collection. Photograph: © The Fine Art Society.
11. Exhibition poster, 1920, lithograph, 75.8 × 47.1 cm, Victoria and Albert Museum, London (Prints, Drawings & Paintings Collection). Photograph: © Victoria and Albert Museum, London.

12. *In the Coulisses – Behind the Scenes*, 1921, signed and inscribed 'In the Coulisses', oil on panel, 63 × 57 cms. Falmouth Art Gallery, Presented to the Corporation of Falmouth in 1923 by Alfred A. de Pass, in memory of his sons [FAMAG: 1923.2]. Photography courtesy Falmouth Art Gallery.

13. *Carnaval*, 1920, oil on canvas, 101.6 × 132.6 cm, Manchester Art Gallery, UK. Photograph courtesy Manchester Art Gallery, UK / Bridgeman Images.

14. *Vanda Evina in Les Roses*, 1924, pen and ink, 35.8 × 25 cm, Victoria and Albert Museum, London (Theatre and Performance Collection). Photograph: © Victoria and Albert Museum, London.

15. Laura Knight at the Circus, 1928. Unattributed photograph in *The Graphic*, 28 January 1928. © Illustrated London News Ltd/ Mary Evans.

16. *The Three Clowns*, 1930, oil on canvas, 77 × 63.5 cm, New Walk Museum & Art Gallery, Leicester, UK (purchased from the artist, 1934). Photograph: © Leicester Arts & Museums / Bridgeman Images.

17. *The Rosinbacks*, 1930, oil on canvas, 78 × 63.5 cm. Photograph: © The Potteries Museum & Art Gallery.

18. *Bareback Rider*, 1935, etching, 25.4 × 12.4 cm, private collection. Photograph: © The Fine Art Society.

19. Two 'Bizarre' side plates from the 'Circus' series, depicting two performing horses, and three clowns, 1934, ceramic. Private Collection / Photograph: © Christie's Images / Bridgeman Images.

20. *Early Morning at a Gypsy Camp*, n.d, oil on canvas, 99 × 153 cm, private collection. Photograph © The Fine Art Society.

21. *The Gypsy*, exhibited 1939, oil on canvas, 61 × 40.6 cm, Tate, Presented by the Trustees of the Chantrey Bequest 1939 © Tate, London 2019.

22. *Land Army Girl*, c.1944, charcoal, pencil and watercolour on board, The National Archives, London.

23. *Corporal JDM Pearson, GC, WAAF*, 1940, oil on canvas, 91.4 × 60.9 cm, Imperial War Museum [Art.IWM ART LD 626]. © Imperial War Museum.

24. *In for Repairs*, 1942, oil on canvas, 101.5 × 127 cm, Harris Museum and Art Gallery, Preston, Lancashire, UK. Photograph: © Harris Museum and Art Gallery, Preston, Lancashire, UK/ Bridgeman Images.

25. *A Balloon Site, Coventry*, 1943, oil on canvas, 102.5 × 127 cm, Imperial War Museum [Art.IWM ART LD 2750]. © Imperial War Museum.

26. *Ruby Loftus Screwing a Breech-Ring*, 1943, oil on canvas, 86.3 × 101.9 cm, Imperial War Museum [Art.IWM ART LD 2850]. © Imperial War Museum.

27. Laura Knight at the 166th RA Summer Exhibition, 1934: Dame Laura Knight standing in front of her painting *Lamorna Birch and his Daughters* in Gallery IV on Members' Varnishing Day and discussing it with (left to right) Harold Knight ARA, Frederick William Elwell ARA, Melton Fisher RA, Sydney Lee RA, Sir Frank Short RA, Richard Jack RA, Sir David Young Cameron RA, Apr 1934. Taken by an Unidentified photographer working for Topical Press Agency Ltd. © Royal Academy of Arts, London.

About the author

Alice Strickland is a curator for the National Trust in London and the South East. Her doctorate considered British women war artists of the Second World War and she has been awarded a Paul Mellon research grant for a publication on women war artists of the First World War. Her other publications include: *Learning from the Masters*, Matthew Potter (ed.), Ashgate (2013) and *Ethel Gabain, Evelyn Gibbs and Evelyn Dunbar: Three approaches to professional art practice in interwar Britain*, and *Women's Contribution to Visual Culture Between the Wars 1918–1939*, Karen Brown (ed.), Ashgate (2008).

Acknowledgements

I would like to thank the many individuals, museums, galleries and picture libraries who have provided images and given permission for works in their collections to be illustrated in this publication, including Maddie Beeson at Imperial War Museums, Jennifer Camilleri at the Royal Academy, Sally Donovan at the National Museum Wales, Patrick Duffy at The Fine Art Society, Luci Gosling at the Mary Evans Picture Library, Katie Herbert at Penlee House Gallery & Museum, Shannyn Johnson at the Canadian War Museum, Freya Levett at the Victoria and Albert Museum, Rob Lloyd at Bridgeman Images, Aidan McNeill at ArtUK, Lisa Olrichs at the National Portrait Gallery, Samantha Richardson at The Potteries Museum & Art Gallery, Natalie Rigby at Falmouth Art Gallery and Fintan Ryan at Tate Images.

I am grateful to John Croft for his consummate knowledge about the life of his Great Aunt and for his advice on the text. I would also like to thank Professor Sam Smiles for his long standing encouragement and Greg for his loving support. Finally, I would like to dedicate this book to all the amazing women in my life, most especially Freya, Jane and Vee.

Laura Knight
by Alice Strickland
First Edition

First published in the United Kingdom in 2019 by Eiderdown Books.
eiderdownbooks.com

Series conceived and developed by Eiderdown Books.
Text copyright © Alice Strickland and Eiderdown Books, 2019.
Images copyright © Reproduced with permission of
The Estate of Dame Laura Knight DBE RA 2019. All Rights Reserved.
Additional copyright permissions: see Image credits.

The moral right of the author has been asserted.

All rights reserved. No part of this publication may be reproduced,
stored in a retrieval system, or transmitted in any form or by any means,
electronic, mechanical, photocopying, recording or otherwise, without the
prior written permission from the publisher and copyright owners.

Every effort has been made to ensure images are correctly
attributed however if any omission or error has been made please
notify the publisher for correction in future editions.

A CIP catalogue record for this book is available from the British Library.

ISBN: 978-1-9160416-3-9

Series Editor: Katy Norris
Editor: Rebeka Cohen
Indexer: Hilary Bird
Series design by Clare Skeats
Typeset by Clare Skeats in Lelo by Katharina Köhler

The Modern Women Artists logotype is set in Hesse Antiqua,
which was released in 2018 to mark the 100th birthday of
Gudrun Zapf von Hesse. The forms of Hesse Antiqua are based
on the metal punches that von Hesse created in 1947, while working
as a bookbinder at the Bauer Type Foundry in Frankfurt.

Printed and bound by Imago
Reprographics by ALTA